# MODERN
# INDIAN
# HISTORY

*Key Issues in Asian Studies, No. 23*

**AAS Resources for Teaching About Asia**

# MODERN INDIAN HISTORY

## EMILY ROOK-KOEPSEL

Association for Asian Studies, Inc.
825 Victors Way, Suite 310
Ann Arbor, MI 48108 USA
www.asianstudies.org

# KEY ISSUES IN ASIAN STUDIES

"Key Issues" volumes complement the Association for Asian Studies' teaching journal, *Education About Asia*—a practical teaching resource for secondary school, college, and university instructors, as well as an invaluable source of information for students, scholars, libraries, and those who have an interest in Asia.

Formed in 1941, the Association for Asian Studies (AAS)—the largest society of its kind, with close to 6,000 members worldwide—is a scholarly, non-political, non-profit professional association open to all persons interested in Asia.

**For further information, please visit www.asianstudies.org**

Copyright © 2024 by the Association for Asian Studies, Inc.

Published by the Association for Asian Studies, Inc. All Rights Reserved. Written permission must be secured to use or reproduce any part of this book.

**AAS books are distributed by Columbia University Press.**

For orders or inquiries, please visit https://cup.columbia.edu

Cataloging-in-Publication (CIP) Data is available from the Library of Congress.

*This book is dedicated to Lucien Ellington,
a champion for enhancing student understanding of Asia
and building bridges between colleges, universities, and schools.*

# About "Key Issues in Asian Studies"

*Key Issues in Asian Studies* (*KIAS*) volumes engage major cultural and historical themes in the Asian experience. *Key Issues* books complement the Association for Asian Studies' teaching journal, *Education About Asia*, and serve as vital educational materials that are both accessible and affordable for classroom use.

*Key Issues* books tackle broad subjects or major events in an introductory but compelling style appropriate for survey courses. Although authors of the series have distinguished themselves as scholars as well as teachers, the prose style employed is accessible for broad audiences. This series is intended for teachers and undergraduates at two- and four-year colleges as well as advanced high school students and secondary school teachers engaged in teaching Asian studies in a comparative framework and anyone with an interest in Asia.

**For further information visit www.asianstudies.org.**

**"Key Issues" volumes available from AAS:**

- *Japanese Government and Politics* / Lauren McKee
- *Shintō in the History and Culture of Japan* / Ronald S. Green
- *Indonesia: History, Heritage, Culture* / Kathleen M. Adams
- *The Philippines: From Earliest Times to the Present* / Damon L. Woods
- *Chinese Literature: An Introduction* / Ihor Pidhainy
- *The Mongol Empire in World History* / Helen Hundley
- *Japanese Literature: From Murasaki to Murakami* / Marvin Marcus
- *Japan Since 1945* / Paul E. Dunscomb
- *East Asian Societies* / W. Lawrence Neuman
- *Confucius in East Asia* / Jeffrey L. Richey
- *The Story of Việt Nam: From Prehistory to the Present* / Shelton Woods
- *Modern Chinese History* / David Kenley
- *Korea in World History* / Donald N. Clark
- *Traditional China in Asian and World History* / Tansen Sen & Victor Mair
- *Zen Past and Present* / Eric Cunningham
- *Japan and Imperialism, 1853–1945* / James L. Huffman
- *Japanese Popular Culture and Globalization* / William M. Tsutsui
- *Global India ca 100 CE: South Asia in Early World History* / Richard H. Davis
- *Caste in India* / Diane Mines
- *Understanding East Asia's Economic "Miracles"* / Zhiqun Zhu
- *Political Rights in Post-Mao China* / Merle Goldman
- *Gender, Sexuality, and Body Politics in Modern Asia* / Michael Peletz

# About the Author

**EMILY ROOK-KOEPSEL** is the assistant director for academic affairs at the University of Pittsburgh's Asian Studies Center. Her teaching and research interests focus on gender, caste, and democracy in modern India. Her recent publications include *Democracy and Unity in Modern India: Understanding the All India Phenomenon, 1940–1960* (Routledge, 2019) and articles about gender and minority citizenship in *South Asia: Journal of South Asian Studies* and the *Journal of Women's History*. She is currently researching civil disobedience and democracy in postcolonial India.

# Contents

About the Author / vii

List of Illustrations / xi

Acknowledgments / xiii

Editor's Introduction / xv

Modern Indian History: A Timeline / xvii

Map of India / xix

Introduction: What Is India? / 1

**Chapter 1:** Modern India and the Mughal Empire / 5

**Chapter 2:** The Rise of British Colonialism in India / 15

**Chapter 3:** India and the British Empire / 25

**Chapter 4:** Indian Nationalism to World War II / 35

**Chapter 5:** Independence, Partition, and a New Indian State / 47

**Chapter 6:** Reorganization and Reconstruction
of Indian Life, 1950–1965 / 57

**Chapter 7:** Political Change, Environmental Change, 1966–1985 / 69

**Chapter 8:** India in a New Century, 1985–2010 / 79

Conclusion: Being Indian in the Twenty-First Century / 87

Notes / 91

Glossary / 103

Suggestions for Further Reading / 107

# List of Illustrations

**Figures**

1.1. The Taj Mahal, a Mughal tomb, an important site for Indian tourism / 6

1.2. Akbar I (1542–1605) / 9

1.3. View of Akbar's Palace at Fatehpur Sikri / 12

1.4. Jantar Mantar in Delhi / 12

1.5. An example of Mughal miniature painting / 13

2.1. Dutch Factory in Bengal / 17

2.2. The British East India Company's Fort George in Madras (Chennai) / 18

2.3. Painting of Fort William in Calcutta by the artist Jan Van Ryne in 1754 / 19

2.4. A British East India Company officer in the style of a Mughal ruler, made around 1760 / 21

3.1. A statue of Jotiba Phule teaching Indian feminist and educationist Savitribai Phule at Phulewada in Pune / 27

3.2. Delegates to the first meeting of the Indian National Congress, 1885 / 29

3.3. Attendees at the All-India Muslim League Conference, 1906 / 29

3.4. Image of Bharat Mata (Mother India) by Abanindranath Tagore / 31

4.1. Mahatma Gandhi and his Wife, Kasturba Gandhi, on their voyage from South Africa to India in 1915 / 37

4.2. *Bombay Chronicle*, a daily newspaper, advertisement for noncooperation movement actions / 39

4.3. Dr. Bhimrao Ambedkar / 41

4.4. Gandhi on his way to Dandi during the Salt March / 43

5.1. Indian troops arriving on an Allied base in Singapore in 1941 / 48

5.2. Quit India procession in Bangalore, 1942 / 50

5.3. Special trains ran from India to Pakistan and from Pakistan to India, transporting refugees / 53

6.1. Dignitaries at the First Republic Day Parade in 1950, including B. R. Ambedkar, the drafter of the constitution  /  58

6.2. A woman coming to vote in New Delhi, 1952  /  59

7.1. Indira Gandhi in 1961  /  71

7.2. The Golden Temple in Amritsar  /  77

8.1. Babri Masjid, before it was demolished by rioters in 1992  /  83

8.2. Statues of Mayawati and Kanshi Ram at Ambedkar Park in Lucknow  /  85

8.3. Protesting section 377, which criminalized homosexuality in India, in 2018  /  86

**Maps**

1.1. The Mughal Empire in 1605  /  7

1.2. The Mughal Empire in 1700  /  8

2.1. Map of trade routes throughout Asia  /  16

3.1. Map of the 1905 partition of Bengal  /  30

5.1. Map of the partition of India into India and Pakistan  /  52

6.1. Map of Indian states and territories and their primary languages  /  62

6.2. Map of Kashmir, showing the Line of Control and disputed areas  /  66

7.1. Map of South Asia, 1960s, with Pakistan highlighted  /  74

# Acknowledgments

This book could not have been written without the support of several people and institutions. I sincerely appreciate the University of Pittsburgh's Asian Studies Center and its staff for their daily encouragement and material support while I was writing this book. I very significantly underestimated both the time and difficulty involved in writing a very short introduction for high school and college students, and my manuscript required significant revision and rethinking. Lucien Ellington, the editor of this series, read and reread each part of this manuscript several times, patiently and productively making this book more readable and better considered each time. I appreciate his thoughtful comments and bracing manner, as well as his willingness to continue on with the project even on its third or fourth iteration. Little did I know when taking on this assignment that it would be Lucien's final project. Lucien passed away suddenly and unexpectedly in May of this year. Lucien was an excellent scholar, editor, and supporter of Asian Studies, and will be missed. I also want to thank the anonymous reviewers of the text who meticulously read through the document, and whose comments invariably made the manuscript considerably better. In the same vein, I thank my friends and colleagues who looked at parts of this book as it was in production.

In part, I undertook this project to ensure that I had a short book on Indian history, something I care deeply about, to give to my sons, Robert and Simon. The two of them, and my husband, Abe, are my reason for most things and my best, strongest, and most consistent support. I thank them from the bottom of my heart.

# Editor's Introduction

This volume is a valuable and practical contribution to the AAS Key Issues in Asian Studies series. Emily, in a brief introduction, makes readers aware of India's paradoxes; then, beginning with the latter part of the Mughal Empire and ending with contemporary India, she provides high school students, undergraduates, educators, and general readers with a basic but interesting treatment of the world's most populous nation and democracy. Emily's book is not impeded by the overuse of "academic" language that detracts from reader engagement in what should ideally be true in all Key Issues volumes—a good story.

This volume is a good story about India. I am now convinced India is the most diverse major nation and, perhaps, the most diverse nation in the world. The United States and the People's Republic of China are diverse but, in my opinion, less so than India. Readers focusing upon Asia will certainly be positioned to challenge or support my contention if they read both Emily's volume and David Kenley's Key Issues volume, *Modern Chinese History*.

Languages and religions constitute two of many levels included in Emily's book. Based upon India's constitution and a recent census, India has twenty-two "scheduled" languages out of a total of 121 languages recognized as "mother tongues" that constitute the first language a child learns. Hundreds of other languages are spoken throughout India. Most North American readers do not associate India with Christianity. Christians constitute less than 5 percent of 1.4 billion Indian citizens, but this means there are seventy-one million Indian Christians—more adherents than in most Western European countries. Mother Teresa, perhaps the world's most famous Christian, was a naturalized Indian citizen for well over half her life.

Despite my best efforts, for nine years, I was unable to successfully find a historian of India who would commit to writing a brief volume on the subcontinent and follow through on the commitment. Emily is the notable exception. She accepted the challenge, persevered, and has produced an excellent Key Issues volume.

Although no volume—especially one about India—will please every reader, what warms my heart the most about this volume is that Emily made sure with controversial topics that readers benefited from "a marketplace of ideas." In the AAS Asia Shorts series, authors are free to publish volumes with ideological perspectives since the series is designed for upper-level readers. My objective, considering the age and knowledge level of our readers, beginning with the first Key Issues volume was, through "position diversity," to not teach Key Issues readers *what* to think but rather *how* to think. I did my best!

As is the case with every volume, this Key Issues volume would not have been possible without the hard work of several other people. Michele Louro read and commented upon the original proposal. Nimish Adhia and Chandar Sundaram reviewed and made valuable suggestions that helped improve the manuscript. My graduate student Savannah Mason, who is much closer to the typical Key Issues reader's age than anyone else mentioned in this introduction, was especially helpful with the volume. I am especially grateful to the AAS Editorial Board and particularly the chair, Jan Bardsley, for their support of Key Issues in Asian Studies throughout the years. Last but not least, I am grateful to AAS Publications Manager Jon Wilson for his consistent support and friendship for over thirty years.

*Lucien Ellington*

# Modern Indian History
## A Timeline

| | |
|---|---|
| 1526 | Founding of the Mughal Empire in India |
| 1600 | British East India Company founded to control British trade with India |
| 1686 | First Anglo-Mughal War |
| 1707 | Mughal Empire at its height of power and area |
| 1764 | British East India Company wins the Battle of Buxar against Mughal forces; British East India Company granted control over the province of Bengal |
| 1857–1859 | First War for Indian Independence; after defeating Indian forces, the British government dissolves the British East India Company's governing powers and adds India to the British Empire. |
| 1885 | Indian National Congress founded |
| 1905 | First partition of Bengal; beginning of the Swadeshi movement |
| 1906 | Founding of the All-India Muslim League |
| 1915 | Mohandas "Mahatma" Gandhi returns to India from South Africa, begins anti-colonial agitations |
| 1920–1922 | Noncooperation movement |
| 1930 | Congress declares full independence as goal; Gandhi completes the Salt March |
| 1942 | Congress begins the Quit India movement targeted on the British government leaving India |
| 1947 | India is partitioned into India and Pakistan; India and Pakistan declared independent |
| 1948 | First Indo-Pak War; Line of Control established in Kashmir; Mahatma Gandhi assassinated |

| | |
|---|---|
| 1950 | Indian constitution is ratified |
| 1962 | Sino-Indian War |
| 1965 | Second Indo-Pak War |
| 196 | Start of the Green Revolution in India |
| 1971 | Third Indo-Pak War; Bangladesh becomes independent; J. P. Narayan begins the Total Revolution movement |
| 1975–1977 | Indira Gandhi declares emergency in India, political and civil rights suspended |
| 1991 | Economic liberalization measures are passed to open India's economy |
| 1992 | Hindu nationalists tear down the Babri Masjid in Ayodhya; communal rioting throughout India |
| 2002 | Communal riots break out in Gujarat, killing hundreds |
| 2014 | Narendra Modi is elected prime minister of India |
| 2024 | India passes China to become the most populous nation in the world |

# MAP OF INDIA

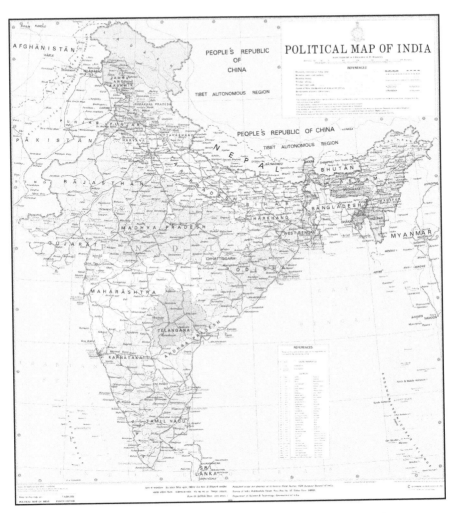

2019 Political Map of India, published by the Press Information Bureau on behalf of the Ministry of Home Affairs, Government of India under the Release ID 1590112 https://static.pib.gov.in/WriteReadData/ userfiles/India%20%20Political2.pdf

# Introduction

# What is India?

India is often described in broad strokes. It is called the world's largest democracy, an ancient civilization, and the birthplace of many world religions. These brief descriptions tie modern-day India to a proud, long-standing and rich history, culture, and political society. Standing alongside these statements are images of India as a poor, unstable, violent, and occasionally authoritarian state that appear in newspaper articles, histories, and travelogues. For every image of crowds celebrating holidays or peacefully standing in line to cast a ballot, there are pictures of violent rioting and undernourished children. The story of India combines all these ideas and many more as well. India cannot be described as a single, static story. It is a complicated and diverse nation with a complicated and diverse geography and people.

India, as a modern nation-state, has been and continues to be at the crossroads of regional, demographic, and political changes. It is the major regional power of a strategically critical, and often politically and environmentally unstable, South Asian region. In 2023, India became the most populous nation in the world, home to more than 1.4 billion people, approximately one-sixth of the world's population. Home to more than one hundred languages, several different indigenous populations, and strong regional traditions, India relies on the idea of unity in diversity to connect its large population to its national project. India's economy, the world's fifth largest, boasts some of the richest people in the world as well as large amounts of poverty. India is also at the center of several powerful but tenuous relationships with neighboring countries, including existing unsettled border conflicts with Pakistan and China. India is home to several sources of appealing "soft power"; Bollywood, or Hindi-language cinema, is watched and loved around the world, and the global spread of yoga has brought Indian language and Indian practices into homes and lives around the world. Large Indian diaspora communities exist in North America, Western Europe (particularly the UK), and the Middle East. This diaspora creates strong economic connections between India and the rest of the world. For these reasons, knowledge about South Asia, and India in particular, has become important as a marker of global competence.

The Indian subcontinent has a long human history. Archeologists and historians believe organized societies have existed continuously on the Indian subcontinent for more than eight thousand years.[1] India is the birthplace of four major world religions—Hinduism, Sikhism, Buddhism, and Jainism. Because of this long history, colonial and nationalist histories alike have described India as ancient and traditional. Popular images of the country, both in India and in the West, often depict it as unchanging, with deep ties to its complete long history.

This image of India as a single, unified entity spanning the space of the entire South Asian subcontinent solidified only in the twentieth century. Although various regional empires at times consolidated power over large swaths of the Indian subcontinent, the vision of a single government, especially a democratic republic, with power over the entire subcontinent was not a common idea prior to the early twentieth century. When people think about early modern Indian empires or states, like the Mughal Empire, the Vijayanagara Empire, or the Deccan sultanates, they are almost always considering imperial projects that were primarily regional.

As a modern nation-state, though, India is remarkably young. India only achieved independence in 1947, after more than two hundred years of colonial rule. India's constitution only went into effect in 1950. Geographically, the borders of the Indian state remain undefined—India's border with China and Pakistan are both officially unsettled. India's internal geography remains similarly unsettled, with changes to the lists of Indian union territories as recently as 2020.

This concise history of India begins with the Mughal Empire in the sixteenth century and ends with some of the more important twenty-first-century developments. Attention is given to the multiple influences over time that have impacted one of the most culturally and ethnically diverse populations on earth. This book attempts to tell the story of the Indian subcontinent through the lens of many different stakeholders. It is necessary to tell the story of politically powerful Indian elites, and this book will certainly focus on the important role that wealthy and well-connected Hindu reformers, Indian nationalists, and national leaders played in writing the history of India, but it will also look at Indian history from the point of view of political minorities, with a special focus on Dalits, women, and Muslims.

"Dalit" is the contemporary term for the group of people previously called "untouchables," or the "depressed castes or classes." The Indian caste system is a set of hierarchical classifications originally found in a Hindu religious text, the *Rig Veda*, that characterized people based on their birth into four basic strata—called "varnas"—that would define their status in society. Three varna—the Brahmins designated the priestly castes; Kshatriya, the kings or leaders; the Vaishya, the merchants—were the upper castes. Shudras, the fourth varna, were the laborers, and restrictions around their day-to-day lives were significant. Dalits were people who were not born into any of these four varna, and they held the lowest possible status. Because they were not within a varna, Dalit people were considered polluting to Hindus in the varnas. As such, they were often excluded from society, education, and religious rituals of Hindu society. Dalits traditionally were forced into so-called "polluting professions" like sanitation, dealing with remains, leather tanning, and mortuary work. Dalits were not welcome to use public spaces, including drawing water at public wells, praying in temples, or even walking around a city. Forced onto the least productive agricultural lands and into the least profitable jobs, Dalit families have often coupled poverty with discrimination that kept them out of educational institutions and positions of power. Even today, when there are laws banning caste-based discrimination, and policies meant to increase the number of lower-caste and Dalit people in education, politics, and employment, Dalits face systematic discrimination and casteism. Facing an uphill battle in searching for jobs, prejudice in educational settings, and the intersection of discrimination and poverty, Dalits continue to be underrepresented in education and politics.

Women, while making up close to 50 percent of India's population, have often had to fight for equal rights, both under the law and in social situations. Up until the middle of the twentieth century, women were unable to hold jobs after marriage, inherit property equally, or keep custody of their children in a divorce. Women still face discrimination in many areas of Indian society.

India is home to the third-largest Muslim population in the world, and Muslims have been an integral part of Indian society since at least the later part of the seventh century. Yet, many Indians still see Indian Muslims as somehow not really Indian. Indian Muslims continue to be discriminated against and even face violence because of their faith. For these reasons, it is vital to include these Indian narratives as part of any story of modern Indian history.

The history of India is fascinating, complicated, and sometimes difficult. It includes the drive to throw off colonial oppression and the internal oppression of less powerful communities, the move toward legal equality for all people, and the enforcement of societal discrimination. Indian history is also, and most importantly, dynamic and ever changing. I make no claim whatsoever to give a comprehensive treatment of the issues raised in this volume. It is my hope that this basic introduction to India will give readers a sense of this important nation, and that for some readers, it will stimulate a deeper interest in, and desire to learn more about, India.

# 1

## Modern India and the Mughal Empire

### The Mughal Empire: An Introductory Overview

There are several reasons to begin a book about modern Indian history with a chapter on the Mughal Empire, which governed parts of the Indian subcontinent from roughly 1530 until the late eighteenth century. The Mughals were the first rulers of modern India who conceived of themselves as ruling an *Indian* empire. Unlike many of the other sultanates or regional states, the Mughals ruled with an eye toward the larger Indian context and toward consolidating power across the Indian subcontinent. The Mughal Empire's bureaucratic, cultural, and religious policies have continued through India's later history, and they have become—for many but not all Indians—part of India's imagination. One only needs to think about the importance of the world-famous Taj Mahal, a Mughal tomb, to understand how important Mughal history is to the Indian story.

Originally, the Mughals were Muslim Turkic rulers who came to the Indian subcontinent from northwest Asia—from what is now Afghanistan—and then moved southeast across the Gangetic Plains, most of northern and eastern India. By 1530, when the first emperor, Babur, consolidated Mughal holdings into an imperial court, the empire covered the space roughly from modern-day Kashmir in the northwest, to Mewar in the south and the Punjab in the west, and to modern-day Bihar in the east. The Mughal Empire continued to expand for roughly the next one and a half centuries, and at its height around 1707, the Mughal Empire controlled most of what we think of as India today, and much of what we think of as Pakistan and Bangladesh. After 1707, the empire began to decline in both size and power, until it was limited to ceremonial powers, including the granting of titles and stipends, by the first third of the nineteenth century.[1]

Figure 1.1. The Taj Mahal, a Mughal tomb, an important site for Indian tourism.
Source: Dhirad image edited by J. A. Knudson, Wikimedia Commons,
https://commons.wikimedia.org/wiki/File:Taj_Mahal_in_March_2004.jpg.

The Mughal imperial court, first located in Delhi and later relocated to Agra, relied on treaties with regional kings and princes, Mughal-appointed governors, local elites, and military leaders to provide Mughal emperors tributes of goods, armies, and money. Mughal power was largely dependent on the continual expansion of the empire in India. In addition to requiring tribute from regional governments, Mughal rulers also collected taxes on agricultural properties in areas they ruled directly to continue to fund military campaigns and administer the central imperial court. In return for taxes or tribute, the imperial court provided protection from raiders; bureaucratic services like mapping, tax reform, and mediation among regional powers engaged in disputes; and funds toward infrastructure and aid. Mughal rulers consolidated their control and their wealth through relatively constant military campaigns against regional powers but were careful to cultivate strong—and often, though not always, friendly—tributary relationships with defeated princes and military leaders, sometimes including rivals as ministers, court members, or even as wives to create bonds of loyalty.[2] The Mughal emperors supported and proposed new systems of governance and courts that lasted through the modern period into the present day, propagated Persian as a common court language, and were strong supporters of legal reform across India.

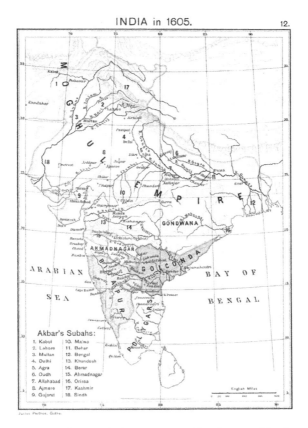

Map 1.1: The Mughal Empire in 1605. Source: Charles Joppen, *Historical Atlas of India* (London: Longmans, Green & Co., 1907), reprinted from Wikimedia Commons, https://commons.wikimedia.org/wiki/ File:India_in_1605_from_%22Historical_Atlas_of_ India,%22_by_Charles_Joppen.jpg.

Although tributary relationships were a primary form of revenue within the empire, by the late 1500s, the Mughal Empire had developed a system of more direct taxation. This policy was coupled with a reform of land usage and ownership known as the zamindari system. Large local landowners (zamindars) were granted certain tax advantages and funds for land-improvement schemes, such as irrigation and waterworks construction. In return, zamindars served the state, collecting taxes from their peasant cultivators and raising and paying troops for Mughal expansion campaigns. Zamindars could be of any religion and were often granted status because of their wealth and local connections. Although there were differences in the zamindari system and European medieval feudalism, strong similarities existed. The zamindar could demand that peasants provide labor,

Map 1.2: The Mughal Empire in 1700. Source:
Charles Joppen, *Historical Atlas of India* (London:
Longmans, Green & Co., 1907), reprinted
from Wikimedia Commons, https://commons.
wikimedia.org/wiki/File:India_in_1700_
from_%22Historical_Atlas_of_India,%22_by_
Charles_Joppen.jpg.

goods, or imperial military service. Mughal cities, court projects, and military campaigns were dependent on agricultural taxes and zamindar participation. As such, Mughal administrators and bureaucrats focused on making sure that zamindari lands were consistently mapped and assessed, that they generally paid their assessed tax, and that they remained loyal to Mughal power.[3]

In addition to constituting a system that supported and reinforced Mughal power, the zamindari system reinforced other power structures in Indian village life. The zamindari system tied caste-based privileges, wealth, and education to landownership, village patronage, and political power. Lower-caste peoples,

Figure 1.2. Akbar I (1542–1605). Source: Wikimedia Commons, https://commons.wikimedia.org/wiki/File:Akbar_the_Great_Mogul,_1542-1605_(1917)_(14586703359).jpg.

particularly Dalits (formerly known as untouchables), often lived on marginal land, were not able to provide significant funds toward the tax, and were expected to contribute free labor to the zamindar. The labor requirement, sometimes as much as a third of a person's time, meant that lower-caste and Dalit peasants were generally unable to break the cycle of poverty. Women were also significantly disadvantaged under the zamindari system. When zamindars saw themselves as the owners of a person's labor, that often meant that the assault or rape of women peasants could be considered part of peasant-labor services, a practice that continued throughout the modern period until the twentieth-century abolition of the zamindari system.

# THE RISE AND FALL OF THE MUGHAL EMPIRE

In 1526, the military leader Babur, the first Mughal emperor, defeated the sultan of Delhi's armies, and by 1530, he secured his conquest. He died soon afterward. Barbur's death set off a period of uncertainty about the continuation of the new empire. By approximately 1565, his teenage grandson Akbar consolidated the power of the Mughal court and expanded its imperial reach, encompassing all of the northern Indian subcontinent. Akbar, later known as the Great Mughal, established diplomatic ties with neighboring kingdoms to the west and south and increased the participation of local kingdoms and military leaders of regionally important tributary partners in his court.

Akbar's court was defined by the practice of making politics, military strength, and culture all equal parts in imperial power. Although he never learned to read or write, Akbar built a cosmopolitan court that was meant to mirror the diversity of the Mughal realm. Akbar shifted the court south from Delhi to Agra (slightly over four hours today by automobile) and encouraged advances in architecture, gardening, painting, music, and religious expression. Akbar's court was also distinctly religiously pluralistic. Muslim, Hindu, and Christian scholars, authors, and critics were employed and encouraged.[4] His court rescinded the extra taxes that non-Muslim citizens paid, and he included Hindu clerics and religious thinkers in discussions of religion. This policy allowed for non-Muslim leaders, thinkers, and artists to be part of the Mughal power structure.

In addition to transforming regional military leaders into Mughal army generals, Akbar made strategic marriage alliances with powerful daughters of regional leaders. These marriages drew regional kingdoms more tightly into the Mughal system of patronage. They also highlighted Mughal court claims that both the imperial family and regional partners enjoyed mutually beneficial relationships.

Akbar's successors, Jahangir (1605–1627) and Shah Jahan (1628–1658), also extended the reach of the empire, focusing on access to Indian Ocean ports in Gujarat—particularly Surat, the most prosperous port in the Mughal Empire—with the idea of increasing Indian Ocean trade between the subcontinent and Western Asia. Shah Jahan also began to consolidate power in the Deccan, a powerful central Indian state with its capital in what is now Hyderabad. Shah Jahan's son Aurangzeb was able to fully incorporate the Deccan into the Mughal Empire and begin to engage in southward and eastward expansion.

Unlike Akbar, Jahangir, or Shah Jahan, Aurangzeb (1658–1707), the last powerful Mughal emperor, was not as interested in maintaining a wide-ranging and diverse court experience. Aurangzeb was both attracted to using military force for imperial expansion and concerned about rising imperial court expenses. He resumed military campaigns and promoted a more austere court. Aurangzeb reinstated the additional tax on non-Muslim citizens of the empire, a move that had financial implications for primarily non-Muslim tributary states and also indicated a shift against the full participation of Hindus, the majority of the Indian population. These changes further alienated non-Muslim tributary partners, such as the predominately Hindu Rajputs and Marathas.

The latter part of Aurangzeb's rule was marked by significant military victories in the south and west against the Deccan princes in central India and the Maratha Empire around the areas of Pune, near the center of India's western coast and Bombay. Yet, it was also a time of rising regional states and a renewal of local and regional power. Even as Aurangzeb won battles in the Indian south, more established parts of the empire were starting to rise against Mughal rule.

After Aurangzeb's death, internal power struggles among his sons and the rise of regional powers led to a gradual disintegration of the ties that had held the empire together. Over time, princes and regional leaders stopped paying taxes and tributes and stopped sending armies for the empire to command. Mughal-appointed provincial governors laid claim to the territories and lands subject to their supervision, and zamindars refused to pay taxes and tributes to their imperial intermediaries. Declining revenues and smaller imperial armies meant that the expansion of the empire was no longer possible, and seeing declining imperial power, tributary partners continued to break away from the empire.[5]

The Mughal Empire's gradual contraction meant that people began to identify with their regional areas—as Marathas, Rajputs, or Pathans—rather than as part of the Mughal Empire, giving regional states more power. The decline of central Mughal authority and the rise of regional powers created a scramble for power and territory among regional bodies. Some regional powers, like the Rajputs and the Marathas, provided troops to the Mughals but also began to build strong personal armies that they could use to fight against the Mughal army, against other regional powers, or amongst themselves. Regional and local leaders encouraged zamindars in their region to join new coalitions with their revenue and goods rather than send them on to Agra. By the mid-nineteenth century, the Mughal Empire had contracted to purely ceremonial duties with very limited revenue and courts.

## THE MUGHAL EMPIRE IN INDIAN CULTURAL LIFE

By the time the Mughal Empire consolidated itself as the primary political organization on the Indian subcontinent, Mughals and their ancestors had been in India for more than five hundred years. The Mughal courts were generally strong patrons of the arts and sciences across the Indian subcontinent. Many iconic Indian sites were built or supported by the Mughal imperial court. Emperor Shah Jahan built the Taj Mahal as a tomb for his chief wife, Empress Mumtaz Mahal. Other examples of important Mughal sites include the Jama Masjid, or "Friday Mosque," in Delhi, the red forts in both Agra and Delhi, the Shalimar Gardens (now in Pakistan), and the court town of Fatehpur Sikri, just outside Agra.[6]

The Mughals funded scientific research, building reputations in the fields of waterworks; agricultural trade and organization; the machinery of war—

Figure 1.3. View of Akbar's palace at Fatehpur Sikri. Source: Wikimedia Commons, https://commons.wikimedia.org/wiki/File:Panoramic_vie_of_ Fahpur_Sikri_Palace.jpg.

especially in gun and cannon design; and other basic sciences.[7] Beginning with Babur, the Mughal imperial court sustained a deep interest in astronomy, and Mughal-supported scientists contributed several hundred astronomical tables to the general understanding of the positioning of the stars. The Mughal imperial court also helped to fund Rajasthani Maharaja Jai Singh II's construction of the five astronomical observatories called Jantar Mantar—roughly translating to "instruments of calculation"—located in Jaipur, Delhi, Varanasi, Ujjain, and Mathura, and each featuring large astronomical devices.

Mughal emperors also supported regional artistic traditions and encouraged the blending of local art and literature practices across the country. Mughal patronage is widely considered to have revived North Indian (Hindustani) classical music and reimagined artistic forms like miniature painting. At its height in the late sixteenth and seventeenth centuries, the Mughal court used its patronage of

Figure 1.4. Jantar Mantar in Delhi. Source: Photo by Gerd Eichmann, Wikimedia Commons, https://commons.wikimedia.org/ wiki/File:Jaipur-Jantar_Mantar-02-2018-gje.jpg.

Figure 1.5. An example of Mughal miniature painting. Source: Wikimedia Commons, https://commons.wikimedia.org/wiki/ File:Da%27ud_Receives_a_Robe_of_Honor_from_Mun%27im_ Khan_-_Google_Art_Project.jpg.

regional music, visual arts, and vernacular literatures as another tool to gain and keep support from tributary partners.

Cultural power, along with marital alliances and tolerant stances on religious practices across the subcontinent, allowed for tributary states and partners to more fully commit to Mughal rule instead of building competing regional partnerships that could challenge imperial control. Even during the eighteenth and early nineteenth centuries, a period of contraction and loss of power for the Mughal Empire, the greatly diminished Mughal court was still influential in directing the politics of trade, regional participation, and cultural preservation, especially in Northern India.[8] The entrance of European trading companies and shipping, the shifting role and expectations of armies, and the rethinking of what it meant to be Indian shaped the end of the Mughal period in India.

# 2

## THE RISE OF BRITISH
## COLONIALISM IN INDIA

Traders from the Arab world began establishing and taking advantage of existing Indian Ocean trade routes as early as the seventh century CE, setting up deep ties between Western Asia, North Africa, and the Indian subcontinent. Traders moved goods between the routes but also spread religious traditions, people, languages, foods, and cultural traditions. Western Indian ports like Cochin (now called Kochi) and Bombay (now called Mumbai) have strong connections to Islamic, Judaic, and Zoroastrian religious traditions, largely because of the ongoing Indian Ocean trade.[1] Similarly, the overland Silk Roads that connected South Asia with East Asia, and maritime trade between ports like Macau and Malacca and Eastern Indian ports such as Calcutta (now called Kolkata) and Chittagong, were long-standing sources of the movement of goods, ideas, and people in the early modern world. Most of these trade routes predated the rise of the Mughal Empire and continued after the rise of European colonialism on the subcontinent, making them an abiding factor in Indian life over many centuries. Indeed, the contemporary flow of labor and goods from India to the United Arab Emirates (UAE), and the remittances that flow back into India from guest workers in the UAE, are an extension of the early modern trade routes and trade connections between Western Asia and the subcontinent.[2]

In the early sixteenth century, the Mughal court began to impose more stringent regulations on the Indian Ocean trade and offered royal permissions for specific traders, in attempting to fight Indian Ocean piracy. Although Greco-Roman trade with the subcontinent had existed in ancient and early world history, the sixteenth century marks a renewal and expansion of European interest in formal trade relationships in India. Between the sixteenth and nineteenth centuries, European trading companies, especially the British East India Company, became regional power brokers in India, building up mercenary armies and wielding political influence both within and against the Mughal state. By the 1850s, the British East

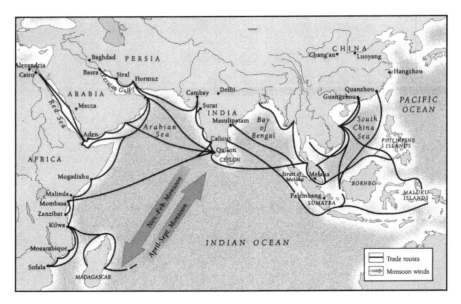

Map 2.1. Map of trade routes throughout Asia. Source: Wikimedia Commons, https://commons.wikimedia.org/wiki/File:Muslim_countries_Trade_k.jpg.

India Company had effectively become a colonizing power throughout much of India, and after the 1857 revolt, official British government rule in India was declared.

## EUROPEAN TRADING POSTS AND INDIAN TRADE

In the sixteenth and seventeenth centuries, European traders began focusing on eastward trade overland through modified and shortened versions of earlier Silk Roads and Indian Ocean trade routes. As early as 1500 CE, Portuguese traders set up factories (what we would call trading posts today) to conduct eastward trade in India. By the mid-sixteenth century, Portuguese traders founded large settlements along the western coast of India, including warehouses and offices in Cochin, Goa, and Bombay. By the early seventeenth century, the Mughal emperor officially approved several other European trading posts, including the French, British, and Dutch East India Companies. Dutch traders were especially strong in the south and east of India. The Dutch, after a short war with the Portuguese, colonized Sri Lanka—then known as Ceylon—and held a near monopoly on the Indian spice trade. The British East India Company was founded in London as a joint-stock company on the last day of 1600, and soon after, it joined the European powers setting up trading posts in various places in India. By the end of the seventeenth century, the British East India Company supported centers of activity in Surat in Gujarat, Bombay, Madras (now called Chennai), and Calcutta. The Portuguese held Goa, and the Dutch and French held Pondicherry.[3]

Figure 2.1. Dutch Factory in Bengal. Source: Wikimedia Commons, https://commons.wikimedia.org/wiki/Commons:Featured_pictures/ Historical#/media/File:De_handelsloge_van_de_VOC_in_ Hougly_in_Bengalen_Rijksmuseum_SK-A-4282.jpeg.

Relations between the European trading posts and settlements and their Mughal hosts were not always friendly. Early in the 1620s, the British East India Company began to create large company-controlled mercenary armies to protect and support their trading outposts, with significant forces in Bombay and Surat. The British East India Company employed soldiers from around Europe and large number of Indians. Indian soldiers (called sepoys) were generally paid less, given fewer opportunities to advance, and were forced to live in less comfortable spaces than European soldiers employed by the Company. The British focused on expanding the company control over lands granted to them within their right to trade in the Mughal Empire. The British East India Company began intervening militarily in disputes between local and regional political powers, and especially in disputes between regional powers challenging the Mughals. The British East India Company's actions put them on a military collision course with the Mughal Empire.

The first Anglo-Mughal war began in 1686 as a trade dispute. The company wanted to trade more widely and pay fewer taxes in their trade with the Mughal Empire and its client provinces. When the negotiations broke down, the Mughal imperial court increased, rather than decreased, the company's tax rate for trade in Bengal. The company responded to the increased tax rate by capturing Chittagong, a regionally important port city, and attempting to take over the whole of Bengal. When the company's attack failed, the Mughal court seized the British East India

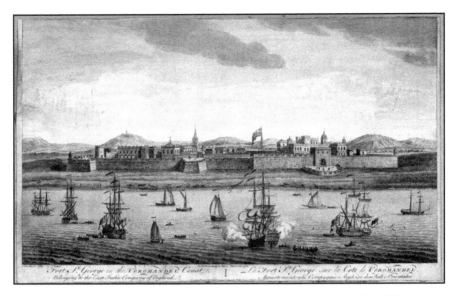

Figure 2.2. The British East India Company's Fort George in Madras (Chennai). Source: Wikimedia Commons, https://commons.wikimedia.org/wiki/File:Fort_St._George,_Chennai.jpg.

Company's trading posts across India, including besieging the company's Bombay garrison for fifteen months. In the end, the company was forced to relent, agree to trading terms set by the Mughal court, and pay a significant fine. Although the war ended in 1690, it foreshadowed the British East India Company's ambition to significantly control India's economy and land. In the several years after the war, the British East India Company did not openly fight with the Mughal court. In their strongholds of Bombay, Surat, and Chittagong, the company began to act more and more like a colonial power, exerting control over the day-to-day functioning of their regions, making new laws, and levying taxes, often without Mughal approval. The company also began building and training a larger army (including Indian soldiers), encouraging regional disputes that destabilized Mughal control, and building physical fortifications around their trading settlements.[4]

## EXPANSION OF THE BRITISH EAST INDIA COMPANY

In 1717, the Mughal emperor Farrukh-Siyar granted the British East India Company tax-free trade in Bengal in exchange for a modest annual tribute to the Mughal court. Tax-free trading made it nearly impossible for other European trading companies, who still paid taxes on their Bengali trade, to compete with the British in Bengal. It also meant that local zamindars, Mughal nobles, and the ruler (nawab) of Bengal province lost important tax revenue. Because of their tax-free status, the British East India Company shifted the center of its operations to Calcutta, the largest city in Bengal. The company built an impressive fort, Fort

Figure 2.3. Painting of Fort William in Calcutta by the artist Jan Van Ryne in 1754. Source: "A Perspective View of Fort Williams," Jan Van Ryne, Wikimedia Commons, https://commons.wikimedia.org/wiki/File:%22A_Perspective_View_of_Fort_William%22_by_Jan_Van_Ryne,_1754.jpg.

William, on the Hooghly River in Calcutta and set themselves up as the mediators of trade in Bengal, further irritating the ostensible ruler of Bengal, who saw the fort as an indication of the company's expansionary goals.[5] Between the building of an impressive fort in the middle of Calcutta, the expansion of military force in Bengal Province, and the tax-free trading dispensation in Bengal granted by the Mughal Empire, the ruling family of Bengal Province began to see the British East India Company as an invading force.

Siraj ud-Daulah, Nawab of Bengal, was right to feel concerned about the British build-up of forces in his province. By the mid-1750s, the British East India Company had amassed large militia forces of Indian soldiers and British officers in Bengal and Madras. In 1756, the British East India Company ignored an order from the nawab of Bengal to disband their military forces. Faced with open defiance, the Bengali army, along with the French East India Company's militia, marched on Fort William and defeated the British East India Company's militia. The British quickly retaliated and brought troops up from Madras, led by Robert Clive, to retake the fort, which they did at the 1757 Battle of Plassey. This British victory forced the French out of Northern India and began several years of skirmishes and battles between the British East India Company and Mughal forces in Bengal and the neighboring states of Oudh and Bihar. In 1764, the British East India Company won a decisive battle at Buxar, causing the Mughal emperor to sue for peace.[6] Through the next several years, in addition to fights with the Mughal Empire, the British East India Company also fought wars against regional powers,

19

including in Mysore (now called Mysuru) in Southern India, against the Marathas in Western India, and against Sikhs who were primarily located in Punjab in the northwest, which forced the company to grow and maintain huge armies primarily consisting of Indian soldiers.[7]

The middle to late 1700s were a period of serious decline for the Mughal Empire, and the conflict with the British East India Company was only one of several factors that weakened the Mughal regime. The Mughal Emperor Aurangzeb's final campaign was against the Marathas in the Deccan in South and Central India. Shortly after his death, the Maratha Empire, a powerful regional force, retook most of the land that Aurangzeb had conquered and looked toward other powers in their region, setting up skirmishes with the British over their holdings in Bombay. The Mughal court was also challenged in Rajputana in Western India, where, in 1750, they finally lost control over the region. Over the next fifty years, Mughal imperial forces continued to lose battles, and eventually, the Mughal court was unable to support an army. By the time the last Mughal emperor, Shah Alam II, died in 1806, he was being held under virtual house arrest, overwhelmed by the British East India Company in the east and the Maratha Empire in the west.[8]

## THE COMPANY RAJ

The 1765 Treaty of Allahabad granted the British the right to collect taxes in Bengal and the surrounding regions, essentially appointing the British East India Company as the de facto government of Bengal, Bihar, and Orissa (which is today the Odisha State on the Bay of Bengal). The creation of the British East India Company as a governing force during the period from 1765 to 1857 is often referred to as the Company Raj. The word "raj" means "rule," and so "Company Raj" would be "ruled by the company." The Treaty of Allahabad technically designated the British East India Company as the governor of the Bengal Province; the effects of the treaty further diminished Mughal imperial power. By 1856, the company controlled many of the former Mughal lands in North India; was the power broker in several princely states, often against the will of the ruling family in those states; and controlled substantial lands in Southern India, making the British East India Company the de facto government in most of India.

The company significantly expanded its armies, setting up large garrisons in Bombay in the west, Calcutta in the east, and Madras in the south. The company employed Indians as soldiers and lower-level officers while often placing control of regiments and most officer positions in the hands of undereducated, ill-prepared British recruits. Company rule included the daily operation of several regional states, a large army, and significant diplomatic responsibilities, but company decisions were motivated by the creation of profits for shareholders in Great Britain and not the well-being of the people or land they controlled.[9] For example, shortly after the Treaty of Allahabad granted the company the right to collect taxes in Bengal, the British ordered a new survey of the region, identifying sources of

Figure 2.4. A British East India Company officer in the style of a Mughal ruler, made around 1760. Source: Dip Chand, "Portrait of an East India Company Official," Wikimedia Commons, https://commons.wikimedia.org/wiki/File:Portrait_of_East_India_Company_official.jpg.

taxable income that provided company management with a good sense of who would be reliable government partners.

The survey was one of many actions on the part of the company targeted at remaking Indian life and Indian people into good colonial investments for the British. Some of those acts, like the 1793 Permanent Settlement Act of Bengal, reorganized property rights in Bengal by instituting a punishing tax cycle that required taxes be paid in money before the harvest. Failure to pay taxes in a timely manner meant that land would be forfeited to the government to be resold. This tax cycle made it almost impossible for any but the richest Bengalis to hold on to land, which encouraged the consolidation of land into larger tracts under single ownership and increased the landless laborer population. It also redirected cultivators toward cash crops like sugar and indigo rather than food crops like pulses—lentils, beans, and peas—rice, and millet, because the tax needed to be paid in money rather than in crops.[10]

The British East India Company governed through a mix of direct and indirect rule, though it generally focused on indirect rule. Indirect rule meant that, except in cases of company profit, the Company Raj would opt to enforce Indian laws and traditions as the company understood them. But the company's British employees had little knowledge about Indian laws, traditions, and government. Often, preexisting racist and cultural stereotypes of Indian laws and traditions substituted for the actual Indian government—for example, the idea that Indians were constantly preoccupied with religion and ruled by religion-based laws. The Company Raj took the idea of religious dogma dominating law as fact, despite having long experience with the Mughal court, which was not, until the latter part of the empire, governed through a sectarian-based legal system.

In 1802, the British created Fort William College, which was established to educate Indian men for lower-ranking administrative roles in the Company Raj and to help create local and religion-based legal codes. These law codes, also called personal law, defined many aspects of civil law based on a respondent's religion. Thus, a person's religion—and often, caste status—defined rules about marriage, inheritance, and property ownership, among other things. These personal law codes persist in Indian law today and have led to different outcomes for Indians in civil law cases based on their religion.[11] Female inheritance of family property, provisions for alimony, and child custody are still governed by personal law, meaning there can be different outcomes for Hindus and Muslims on these issues. Although many Indians would like to see these laws change, powerful, conservative clerics and religious institutions see them as a way to control the Indian population, and particularly women.

## REACTING TO THE COLONIAL RULE OF THE COMPANY RAJ

The response to the Company Raj in the first century of British rule, first in Bengal and later throughout India, was mixed. Generally, elite Indian men in Bengal saw the British as encroaching on their previously held positions of power and privilege, yet they continued to work within the Company Raj's power structure. Reformers, like Raja Ram Mohan Roy (1772–1833) and others, argued that the British were able to control India because Indians had accepted bad customs and harmful traditions. Reform-minded Indian elites argued that if Indians were willing to change corrupt social practices but not necessarily take up British social norms, they would in time become powerful enough to become independent. These proposed reforms were often focused on crafting a vision of a good Indian, someone who embodied Indian cultural customs, specifically upper-caste Hindu customs, and who rejected what these reformers considered the superstitious, low, or underdeveloped patterns of Indian life.

Conversations about reform were often focused on how women were treated in India. The British regularly pointed to the status of Indian women as a justification for their engagement in India. Reformers in India worked to change norms that limited school access for girls and women, helped to pass laws to ban child marriage, advocated for the removal of caste-based strictures on widow remarriage, and pushed for a ban on the practice of sati (burning a widow alive on their husband's funeral pyre). While increasing school attendance for girls, raising the age of marriage, and banning sati benefited some, the reform movements were generally focused on upper-caste and upper-class ideas of womanhood. Reformers did not seek to change practices that primarily impacted lower-caste and lower-class people, such as zamindari practices that required peasants to work for landowners. Because so much of the reform agenda was focused on upper-caste and upper-class Hindu issues, most of the Indian populations—the lower castes, Dalits, lower classes, and non-Hindus—were often forgotten by both reformers and the British.

Throughout the early 1800s, many Indians began to feel that British control diminished the prospects for most of India's population. The Company Raj changed the language of administration from Persian to English and began to propagate policies that denigrated Indian language, culture, religion, and society. A number of events happened around 1850 to make the general feeling of Indian discontent with the Company Raj grow into a full-fledged revolt in 1857. Many leaders of Indian principalities were angry about the way the British East India Company ran roughshod over princely states, and they were especially angry about the company's practice of annexing Indian princely states, pushing rulers, like Rani of Jhansi and leaders of the Maratha Empire to fight against the British East India Company's rule in India. Many Indians were also annoyed by the ongoing failure of the company to consider their worth as leaders, soldiers, and persons. The well-trained leaders of Indian regiments became especially interested in possible revolt.[12]

There were a few immediate causes of the 1857 revolt, including the British 1856 annexation of the powerful princely state of Awadh, which illustrated the company's disrespect for Indian political states, and the introduction of the Enfield rifle into the Indian army. The Enfield rifle included a cartridge that soldiers had to bite to open, and it was rumored to be lubricated by animal fat, specifically a mixture of cow and pig fat, thus offending the religious sentiments of both Hindus and Muslims. While the Enfield rifle story may or may not have been true, the feeling that the British had little to no respect for the sensibilities and strength of Indian soldiers was reinforced by the rumor.[13]

## 1857 INDIAN REBELLION AGAINST THE COMPANY RAJ

Hostilities against the Company Raj began in March 1857, and by May, hundreds of sepoys (Indian soldiers in the British East India Company army) marched to Delhi and declared military allegiance to Bahadur Shah Zafar, claiming him as the Mughal emperor. This move encouraged mass revolt by British East India Company soldiers and opened a path for leaders of several princely states and regional powers to pledge forces to the fight. The conflict was extremely bloody. Well-trained officers managed both sides of the conflict, working with roughly equivalent arms and local knowledge of the terrain. Moreover, because battle forces were relatively evenly matched, much of the fighting revolved around sieges of cities and forts and the death of civilian residents. Fighting was especially hot around Delhi, Lucknow, Kanpur, and Jhansi, with thousands of civilian causalities on both sides. In the end, the British East India Company was able to marshal new forces from Southern India, where the fighting was less intense, and it eventually defeated Indian forces by the end of 1858. The conflict was dubbed the Sepoy Mutiny by British authors, and a war for Indian independence by Indian nationalists.

Overall, more than one hundred thousand Indian soldiers and civilians and more than forty-six thousand British soldiers and civilians died during the conflict.[14] By 1859, the British had completely retaken control in North India and consolidated their rule in former princely states like Jhansi and Awadh. The events of 1857 did trigger a major change in British rule in India. London dissolved the governing power of the British East India Company and placed the management of the Indian colony as a central government function through the newly formed India Office. The government of India shifted from being a Company Raj to the British Raj—or rule by Britain. This change, in part, shifted the priority of the British government in India from a purely profit-motivated rule to a relationship based on imperial power more broadly defined. The change also firmly entrenched the British imperial government in India. Even before 1857, some UK citizens—generally understood as citizens of Scotland, Wales, Northern Ireland, and England—were beginning to question whether the Company Raj was either right or profitable. After India was named a government asset, ruled not by the company but by the British government, UK citizens were able to rationalize violent and racist components of colonial rule through the belief that colonialism benefitted the colonized rather than the purse of the colonizer, a proposition that most Indian political leaders quickly and comprehensively rejected.

# 3

## INDIA AND THE BRITISH EMPIRE

Indians responded to British colonial rule, often called the British Raj, in several ways. Some tried to reform Indian society and religions in response to British claims that India was backward and needed to modernize. Other reformers argued that Indians did not need to respond to what the British thought of them; other Indians advocated adopting some British social norms but not all of them.

Indians, whether they were advocating for reform, defiance, or assimilation, were often subject to racist and derogatory colonial ideas that they were ignorant, backward, savage, cruel, or lazy. British notions about what it meant to be Indian were taught in schools, emphasized in Indian government policy, and even reinforced by court cases. As a result, even Indians who opposed the colonial state internalized some of these stereotypes about India and its population. The British government treated Indians as unfit for self-rule throughout the nineteenth and early twentieth centuries, citing their religious differences, gender inequalities, and unfamiliar customs as backward and savage. In response to colonial violence and disrespect, Indian nationalist leaders began to push for self-rule.[1]

The British government considered India to be a critical part in Britain's imperial wealth and geopolitical power. It connected Asian and African portions of the empire, was a conduit for global commerce, and acted as a laboratory for political, social, and medical experiments that would later be implemented in Britain, including smallpox variolation, social quarantining during pandemic, and the enforcement of group civil law codes—all practices that were transported back to Britain or to other parts of the British Empire.[2] Most British Raj officials described India's Mughal governments as "Asiatic despotism," and Indian cultures as stuck in "hoary traditions." Many colonizers stereotyped Black and Brown people as lazy and unfit to govern themselves. Karl Marx, coauthor of *The Communist Manifesto*, reflected British cultural perspectives in describing India as out of sync with the modern world, existing in the past in comparison with British life. Many British people justified their rule over India as a tutelage project that might possibly take centuries until Indians could govern themselves.[3]

British authorities in India used a mix of coercive colonial government institutions, including courts, schools, and the civil service, to influence the way Indians thought about themselves and their fitness for self-rule. In Indian schools, children were taught that "a single shelf of a good European library was worth the whole native literature of Indian and Arabia."[4] Indians and British men who wanted a government position in India needed to take the same Indian civil service exam, but—as was the case with American eighteenth-century English colonists— even Indians who earned high scores on the exams or who demonstrated highly competent performance were placed in lower-level positions. Often, British men who scored lower on the exams became their bosses. The courts and legal scholars codified Indian laws directly from ancient religious texts that had not ever been used as codes of law and then wrote pamphlets and legal opinions that characterized Indians and Indian law as backward and savage.

In response to descriptions of themselves as backward, lazy, and savage, late nineteenth-century elite Indians tried to specifically describe their own strengths, often citing India's strong spiritual—primarily Hindu—nature. Many Hindu upper-caste men, as well as Muslim upper-class men, adopted Western styles of dress, food, and language to present themselves as modern. These reformers argued that becoming like the British would make them more able to build businesses and begin to earn positions in the colonial government. Indian women, primarily Hindu but some other upper-class Indian women as well, were expected to be well educated but tied to traditional religious and cultural practices. Early Indian nationalists argued that women needed to protect India's cultural heritage while men adopted Western norms to engage in the colonial government and wider colonial society. At the same time, societal rules governing Indian women's actions became stricter.[5]

## Indian Politics at the Turn of the Twentieth Century

The late nineteenth century saw an emergence of several early nationalist movements that would directly challenge British rule and fight for Indian independence. Beginning in the late 1800s, the growth of social welfare organizations helped create the capacity for political change. During this period, changes in the Indian economy and civil society led activists to begin thinking about India as a nation rather than exclusively or primarily focusing upon their local regions. Social welfare groups emphasizing substantial changes—such as improving women's and girls' education, reforming Hindu practices like the appalling treatment of widows, alleviating poverty, and ending child marriage and prostitution—began to meet and organize throughout India.[6] Moves toward social reform were not just the provenance of the elites in society. In Pune, Jyotirao Phule, a Dalit thinker and social activist, began to write and organize against the caste system; he particularly opposed Hindu society's treatment of lower-caste and "untouchable" men and women. In 1873, he founded the Satyashodhak Samaj (Truth-Seekers Society) to fight for these oppressed groups' rights.[7]

Figure 3.1. A statue of Jotiba Phule teaching Indian feminist and educationist Savitribai Phule at Phulewada in Pune. Phule was a strong advocate for Dalit people, women, and social change. Source: Wikimedia Commons, https://upload.wikimedia.org/wikipedia/commons/f/f6/Jotirao_ Phule_Savitribai_Phule_Phulewada_Pune.jpg

The late nineteenth century also saw the rise and nationalization of Indian media. Newspapers helped to define and spread issues of broad concern for Indians, and they also provided platforms for early nationalist writers and activists to air grievances against British rule.[8] Despite Indians' low literacy rates, newspapers were widely popular. Literate people acted as newspaper readers, sharing the news with entire families or neighborhoods. Similarly, the rise of cinema, beginning in India in the early 1900s, helped create a common set of images, concerns, and ideas. The cinema and film reel images allowed Indians to imagine a larger India that would include them.[9]

At the turn of the twentieth century, Indian business leaders began to organize politically to argue for more opportunities in the private sector. Entrepreneurs, merchants, and other commercial and technological innovators were particularly concerned about legal changes that disadvantaged Indian-owned businesses while protecting British economic interests. British-imposed legal changes in the middle to late nineteenth century meant that Indian manufacturing firms that spanned several locations had to pay significantly more in taxes than purveyors of British imports. As a result, goods made in India were often more expensive than those of British competitors. Some of the largest and richest Indian family firms were able to prosper in the more globally connected marketplace, in part by partnering with British firms who absorbed some of their high costs. Most middle- and small-sized Indian enterprises lacked the market power and capital to emulate the larger firms.[10]

Elite Indians under British rule were also upset about changes in tax laws that required taxes be paid in money rather than in-kind taxes (e.g., cattle or grain) and instituted tax deadlines that did not match the crop seasons. When the British government took over the East India Company holdings in 1857, they had to buy out company stockholders. To meet this obligation, the British government of India passed on tax increases to Indians to pay off the debt the British government incurred procuring India from the company. Additional taxes were levied for government services, including some things wealthy Indians liked, such as the expansion of telegraph and railway systems and the infrastructure of cities and towns, but also many other expenditures that they did not want to spend their money on, like clearing land for British-run plantations and Indian army deployments in colonial conflicts like the 1878 Anglo-Afghan War. Changes in the taxes on small- and middle-sized farms forced many families off their lands. Newly landless families often worked as laborers on their former farms, relocated to cities or towns, or became transient workers. These economic privations generated intense Indian anger over British rule and led to a groundswell of political organizing.

The Indian National Congress (INC) was founded in 1885 and remains one of the two largest political parties today. The INC was the first truly national political body that drew from leaders across the subcontinent, and it was organized as an explicitly political organization that could represent Indian people to the British government of India. Largely, although not exclusively, made up of wealthy, English-educated, high-caste Hindu men in professional positions, the INC advocated for increased Indian representation in government and more respect for Indians. Party leaders primarily responded to restrictions that kept Indian men from the highest positions in government, education, business, and the army, as well as to British condescending slights that extended to even powerful Indian men. Although the INC made some of the first critiques of the colonial government, in the organization's early years, they usually limited their actions to petitioning government officials and interacting with each other at annual conventions.

Elite Indian Muslims, especially in the United Provinces and Punjab, were also beginning to organize social, educational, and political groups for the uplift, protection, and representation of Indian Muslims. In the 1880s, the Hindu reform movement, the Arya Samaj, advocated for what had been a minor Hindu religious practice of veneration of the cow as a religious and political duty for Hindus. Cow-protection campaigns took on anti-Muslim sentiments, leading to tensions between Hindu and Muslim communities and occasional sectarian violence.[11] At the same time that Indian Muslims were feeling under attack by movements like cow protection, Muslim leaders in North India, like Sir Syed Ahmad Khan and Aga Khan III, were building up educational and political organizations meant to strengthen Indian Muslims' standing in society. In 1875, Sir Syed Ahmad Khan helped begin a college for Indian Muslims, which is now Aligarh Muslim University. Political organizing, in part made possible by the college and its students, helped lead to the founding of the All-India Muslim League by the

THE FIRST INDIAN NATIONAL CONGRESS. 1885.

Figure 3.2. Delegates to the first meeting of the Indian National Congress, 1885. Source: Wikimedia Commons, https://commons.wikimedia.org/ wiki/File:1st_INC1885.jpg.

Figure 3.3. Attendees at the All-India Muslim League Conference in 1906. Source: Wikimedia Commons, https://commons.wikimedia.org/wiki/File:All_ India_Muslim_league_conference_1906_attendees_in_Dhaka.jpg.

third Aga Khan in 1906. Key Indian Muslim leaders decided that a permanent political advocacy group to fight for civil and social rights for Indian Muslims was necessary to represent what they felt to be the specific issues Muslims faced as a political minority. The All-India Muslim League was also careful to position itself during the first decade of the twentieth century as an organization committed to working with both the British Raj and the Congress Party.[12]

## Partition of the Bengal Presidency and Effects

By 1910, the previously cordial relationship between the British Raj and the Indian National Congress had soured. In 1904, Lord Curzon, viceroy of India, asked prominent Indian leaders to comment on his proposal to partition the administrative territory of Bengal, including the modern-day states of Bengal, Assam, Orissa, part of the Uttar Pradesh, and most of what today constitutes the nation of Bangladesh. Virtually all Indian leaders responded negatively to the proposal. Bengal was home to Calcutta, capital of the British Raj. It was also a hub for several social and religious movements across several communities. Indian political and economic leaders saw the move as an attempt to disrupt burgeoning Indian reform movements and economic power. The proposed partition also split Bengal along religious lines, creating a new, majority-Muslim administrative district. Because of this, many influential and affluent Indians considered the partition a British strategic move meant to pit Muslims and Hindus against each other. Dismissing the negative response, Curzon went forward with the partition of Bengal along religious lines in 1905.[13]

Two responses to the partition of Bengal proved important to the future of Indian nationalism: the Swadeshi movement, which was begun as a direct response to the partition, and the 1907 INC split between moderates who believed in working with the British government and more radical members who advocated

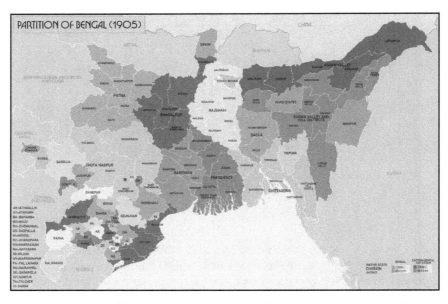

Map 3.1. Map of the 1905 partition of Bengal. Source: XrysD, Wikimedia Commons, https://commons.wikimedia.org/wiki/ File:BengalPartition1905_Map.png.

for home rule. Both responses ultimately served to move the INC and other Indian nationalist movements more generally toward a demand for Indian independence.

Swadeshi is a combination of two Sanskrit words, "*swa*," meaning "own," and "*desh*," meaning "land." The Swadeshi movement called for boycotts of goods produced outside of India, and movement leaders also urged Indians to boycott services, jobs, schools, and other interactions or institutions associated with the British in India. The Swadeshi movement primarily focused on Bengal, although it was active in several other parts of India. Leaders stridently argued that non-Indians had disrupted India's culture and power and that continuing to purchase goods from outside India empowered colonial rulers. The movement was effective in drawing attention to the often negative effects of the British in Indians' daily lives and mobilizing people into thinking, talking, and acting productively toward Indian independence. Still, the movement had several flaws, the most important of which was the Swadeshi movement's reliance on Hindu religious themes, defining Bengal, and by extension India, as a *Hindu* land. Some Swadeshi adherents even labeled Muslims, including those who had lived in India for generations, as outsiders who were no different than the British.[14] Offshoots from the Swadeshi movement encouraged radical protests, both nonviolent and violent, and spurred wider engagement with more extreme positions that exceeded the comfort levels of many INC Party members at the time.

The split in the Congress Party constituted the other major response to the 1907 partition of Bengal. Shortly after the partition, two wings of the Congress Party became embroiled in serious internal conflict. The moderate wing of the party, led by Gopal Gokhale, a professor and social reform activist, argued that although Congress was against the partition of Bengal, the party should first limit responses to petitioning the government for redress. Moderate Congress leaders felt that the more extreme actions hurt economic progress in India. The moderates encouraged a slower, more pro-government set of reforms. The extremist wing of the party, led by Bal Gangadhar Tilak, a newspaper editor, writer, and political leader, saw partition protests and even the revolutionary violence as positive developments toward Indian home rule. Tilak asserted in his newspapers that the Swadeshi movement was an opportunity to build Indian economic strength. Each faction of the Congress Party saw the other as an obstacle for their objectives. The party split in 1907 and was not fully reconstituted until 1916. By then, most of the moderates had changed their positions, and home rule was considered a moderate goal rather than an extreme position, although Congress never supported violent action to help achieve Indian independence.[15]

In 1909, the British government of India introduced a set of reforms, called the Minto-Morley Reforms, intended to quell elite anger about the partition of Bengal. The reforms created more freedom for Indians to participate in government, especially at the provincial level, a longtime Congress objective. The reforms also offered Indian Muslims separate electorates, where only Indian Muslims would vote for candidates for positions in government set aside for Muslims, a very

Figure 3.4. Image of Bharat Mata (Mother India) by
Abanindranath Tagore. In the image, the goddess Mother
India is clearly marked as an upper-caste Hindu woman.
Source: Abanindranath Tagore, *Bharat Mata*, 1905,
Wikimedia Commons, https://commons.wikimedia.org/
wiki/File:Bharat_Mata_by_Abanindranath_Tagore.jpg.

important goal of the All-India Muslim League. Despite these British concessions, virtually all Indian political activists found them unpalatable. The reforms, despite granting more freedom to Indians, excluded Indian political leaders from nationally important political positions, failed to recognize Indian hopes for participation in the upper levels of the army and the civil service, and most critically, failed to reverse the partition of Bengal. The Minto-Morley Reforms were so unpopular that, instead of mollifying Indian opposition to the partition, they solidified both the INC and the All-India Muslim League into pro-home rule positions.

By 1911, after nearly six years of intense protest, the British Indian government reunited much of Bengal by reorganizing the province into linguistic states. Despite the ultimate capitulation of the British, the reunification of Bengal did not end protest movements. Indian political activists had settled on independence as their ultimate objective.

# 4

## INDIAN NATIONALISM TO WORLD WAR II

The early twentieth century was marked by several events that would shape the direction of India's nationalist movements, create several major leaders, and later impact the twenty-first-century political boundaries of Asia. Movements like the Indian National Congress and the All-India Muslim League, among other Indian political organizations, enabled activist members and leaders to begin advocating for more substantial Indian self-determination in the first half of the twentieth century.

Despite coalescing around demands for more autonomy—if not full independence—little consensus existed among Indian political parties on how to achieve these demands. High-profile leaders like Bal Gangadhar Tilak, a more extreme Congress leader, were forceful in their advocacy for home rule and were willing to use political incitement to violence to gain it. Mohandas Gandhi—called "Mahatma," meaning "great soul"—took a different approach and emphasized the value of nonviolence as a means of gaining political and personal autonomy. During the first half of the twentieth century, Indians coalesced around the message that India should be an independent nation.

At the same time, many marginalized groups, including Muslims, Dalits, women, Sikhs, citizens of princely states, and others were attempting to build political constituencies to work within the British colonial government while still advocating for Indian political autonomy. During the first half of the twentieth century, several political organizations, like the All-Indian Muslim League and the Indian Depressed Classes Conference, pushed for separate electorates for minorities in Indian elections while pressuring nationalist parties and the British Indian government to fight for more civil rights, such as temple entry, public wells and water pumps, and entry into schools and colleges.

## WORLD WAR I AND INDIAN NATIONALISM

In 1914, when Great Britain's government officials declared war against Germany and the other Central Powers in World War I, they declared war on behalf of the British Empire, including India. 1.28 million Indian soldiers were widely deployed throughout Africa, the Middle East, and the western front. World War I, especially on the western front, was extremely deadly for all who fought in the trenches, and seventy thousand Indian soldiers died in service.[1] The war harmed India in other ways as well. The British required increased taxes on Indians to help pay for the war. Increased taxes and high levels of inflation meant that more Indians experienced poverty during the war than previously, especially in the agricultural sector, although inflation played a part in temporarily increasing Indian manufacturing.[2] India also faced a series of new emergency civil and economic legislation. The British-imposed Defence of India Acts were meant as wartime restrictions on speech, war profiteering, and other acts but were later continued and strengthened by the British to fight against Indian nationalist movements during the interwar period.[3]

Despite being under new, more onerous restrictions on speech and organizing, Indian political organizations, particularly the Congress and the Muslim League, used the British government's divided attention because of the war to expand their nationalist messages and impact. Earlier, Mohandas Gandhi had left India for England in 1888 to study law. After completing his degree, he went to South Africa to act as an advocate for Indian workers. While in South Africa, Gandhi developed and began to formulate his own nationalist tactics and beliefs, including satyagraha, or nonviolent resistance, and his own conceptualization of swaraj, or self-rule. In 1904, Gandhi began writing and publishing *Indian Opinion*, a newspaper that advocated for nonviolent political action. *Indian Opinion* and several of Gandhi's political pamphlets, first published in South Africa, were also published in India. Although Gandhi did not return to India from South Africa until 1915, his book *Hind Swaraj*, or *Indian Home Rule*, was published and widely distributed in India in 1909.[4] Gandhi's book shifted the position of most Congress Party members to become proponents of at least limited home rule for India, and it helped to change the membership of the organization from an upper-class political petitioning conference to a broader political party that appealed across a wider spectrum of Indians.

In 1915, Gandhi, after building a strong following among Indian nationalists through his publications, returned to India from South Africa and began working with the Congress. Gandhi set up a new ashram (a spiritual or religious community) in Ahmedabad, near Bombay in Western India. From his ashram, Gandhi conducted courses, meetings, and engaged in community organizing that advocated for several causes, including nonviolent resistance. Some of the protests he led included a 1917 campaign in Champaran in Bihar Province in Eastern India, pushing for more rights for landless laborers, and a 1918 campaign in Kheda, near his ashram in Ahmedabad, for tax forgiveness for small farmers

Figure 4.1: Mahatma Gandhi and his wife, Kasturba Gandhi, on their voyage from South Africa to India in 1915. Source: Wikimedia Commons, https://commons.wikimedia.org/wiki/File:Mahatma_ and_Kasturba_Gandhi_on_their_return_to_India_ from_South_Africa_in_1915.jpg.

who were unable to pay land taxes because of recent floods and famines. These actions enabled Gandhi to experiment with tactics and amplify his message of home rule, nonviolent resistance, and community organizing. By the November 11, 1918, armistice that ended World War I, Gandhi had a national reputation and a well-regarded message associated with a newly unified Congress Party.[5]

The war presented a chance for the INC and the All-India Muslim League to find a way to work together for home rule. In 1916, the two organizations held a joint conference in Lucknow, a medium-sized city with a large and relatively important Muslim population in the United Provinces in Northern India. The two organizations demanded greater autonomy and responsibility for Indians in government and the military, as well as a substantial concern for average Indians who were forced to shoulder increasing economic burdens. The authors of the resulting joint resolution, the Lucknow Pact, drafted the strongest set of nationalist demands to date, including Indian-majority membership on all colonial executive councils and legislatures. The joint conference also supported the need for separate electorates for Muslims, something Congress had fought in the past and would fight against in the future. Separate electorates are the right of a given minority group to hold elections among their own population for a legislative seat exclusively reserved for members of that group. Although the alliance would only last for a few years, the Lucknow Pact asserted significant political autonomy as a primary goal of both major political parties in India.

Gandhi's return to India and the political coordination between the Congress and the Muslim League reinvigorated nationalist sentiments throughout India. British officials were aware of the threat Gandhi and his followers posed. In early 1919, only a short time after World War I's November 1918 armistice, the British government reinforced the sweeping restrictions on civil society that had been put in place during the war to try to tamp down nationalist sentiments—with force if necessary. Indians found the restrictions offensive, and their passage sparked nationwide strikes and protests. Between March 30 and April 6, 1919, significant protests occurred in every major Indian city as leaders of major political organizations vowed to disobey the new restrictions.

The protests were particularly heated in the Punjab, leading the British army to enact martial law, banning any further gatherings of Indian residents in the area for any reason. On April 13, 1919, a large group of people congregated at Jallianwala Bagh, a walled garden in Amritsar, a major city in the Punjab. By the end of the day, more than ten thousand people had gathered when British troops, led by General Dyer, blocked the single small entrance and, unprovoked, began firing into the crowd. Almost four hundred people were killed and 1,500 wounded. General Dyer was never punished for this action. The massacre further turned the tide against the British Raj and constituted compelling evidence that disproved in the minds of most Indians the British assertion that government rule was primarily for and by Indians. It also was the impetus for new experiments in nationalist agitation, both against the British and for increased Indian civil and social rights.[6]

## Fighting for a Nation, Theorizing a Nation

The noncooperation movement was an early attempt at nationalism. Launched after the Amritsar massacre, the Gandhi-led civil disobedience Congress Party movement encouraged Indians to actively but peacefully resist what were considered unfair or anti-Indian laws. Widespread boycotts occurred against colonial infrastructure and government, including schools, law courts, the

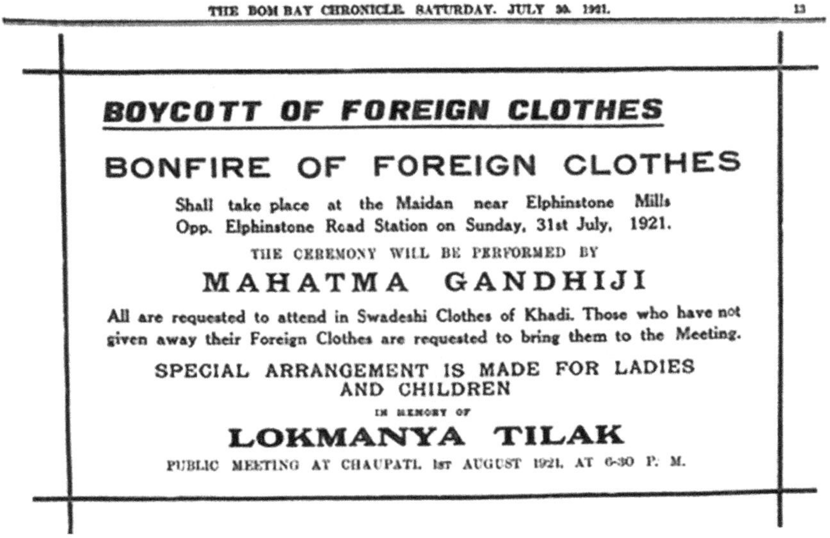

THE BOMBAY CHRONICLE. SATURDAY. JULY 30. 1921. 13

**BOYCOTT OF FOREIGN CLOTHES**

BONFIRE OF FOREIGN CLOTHES

Shall take place at the Maidan near Elphinstone Mills Opp. Elphinstone Road Station on Sunday, 31st July, 1921.

THE CEREMONY WILL BE PERFORMED BY

MAHATMA GANDHIJI

All are requested to attend in Swadeshi Clothes of Khadi. Those who have not given away their Foreign Clothes are requested to bring them to the Meeting.

SPECIAL ARRANGEMENT IS MADE FOR LADIES AND CHILDREN

IN MEMORY OF

LOKMANYA TILAK

PUBLIC MEETING AT CHAUPATI. 1ST AUGUST 1921, AT 6-30 P. M.

Figure 4.2. *Bombay Chronicle,* a daily newspaper, advertisement for noncooperation movement actions. Source: Wikimedia Commons, https://commons.wikimedia.org/wiki/File:Boycott_of_foreign_clothes.jpg.

military, British manufactured items, and railway travel. Indians participating in the noncooperation actions were expected to resist the government without violence and to accept the consequences of their actions, including imprisonment. The movement prompted a more national imagining of India and Indian independence, as people across the country were all working together to protest the colonial infrastructure. Noncooperation threatened the viability of Britain's continued economic and political rule and elevated Gandhi into the national spotlight as the most high-profile anti-British leader.

Noncooperation lasted until February 1922. Gandhi suspended the noncooperation action after a group of villagers attacked a small police station, killing as many as twenty-two police while asserting they were attacking in Gandhi's and Congress's name.[7] Gandhi was arrested for inciting violence and served a short term in jail. He publicly blamed himself for the violence of his followers and went on a three-week purifying fast, urging people to suspend the noncooperation movement until the nation could be obedient to principles of nonviolence and personal responsibility. In 1927, the British appointed the Simon Commission, which was meant to make changes to India's governing documents. The commission did not include any Indian members, nor did the British seem interested in working with Indian political organizations. The Indian response to the Simon Commission was wholeheartedly negative, with many groups boycotting the commission's visit to India. In 1928, Motilal Nehru, father of Jawaharlal Nehru, who later would be a famous nationalist leader and the first prime minister of India, presented a plan, called the Nehru Report, that urged the British to propose dominion status for India—essentially independence—and provided a path for minority representation in any future government. While the Nehru Report was largely ignored, many of its suggestions were reconsidered in the late 1940s when the Constituent Assembly was working on the constitution for an independent India.

Although Gandhi's and Congress's political organization often dominates discussions of the 1920s and 1930s, they were not the only anti-colonial Indian political party during the interwar period. In the early 1920s, the Muslim League organized a protest in support of the caliph, the chief religious and political ruler of Turkey's Ottoman Empire, shortly before the empire's overthrow. Outwardly, the action was seen as a pan-Islamic protest movement, but Muslim organizers within India saw the movement as a chance to connect Indian Muslims to a larger international community of believers who shared a cultural citizenship. This idea of Muslims as both Indian and a part of a larger international community of faith continued to be important in Indian Muslim political organizing throughout the 1920s and 1930s.[8]

The self-respect or anti-Brahmanism movement, one of the most significant movements both politically and socially, started in the early to mid-1920s in Tamil Nadu, a southeastern Indian state. The movement's leader—E. V. Ramasamy, a South Indian lower-caste advocate and politician who also used the name Periyar—argued that lower-caste people deserved as much respect and care as upper-caste people, particularly Brahmans. Periyar contended that to claim political independence, Indian society needed to free itself from the social blight of a caste system that elevated some humans and denigrated others based on their birth status. Self-respect movement leaders were highly skeptical of "freedom fighters" who pushed for freedom from the British as a first step and the elimination of the caste system as a secondary objective. Periyar was particularly critical of Congress and its leaders for this seeming incongruity of words versus actions. The self-respect movement, relatively progressive on gender and class equality, emphasized that if Indians thought of themselves and others as Indian and human, then there should be no intrinsic difference in the worth of any other person.[9]

Additionally, several other anti-caste agitators were becoming nationally important in the middle to late 1920s, including Dr. Bhimrao Ramji Ambedkar, who would become the most recognizable Dalit leader in India fighting social and civil discrimination against Dalit people.

Ambedkar wrote compellingly about the plight of Dalit people, who were unable to participate safely in daily life. His early public movements included campaigns to allow Dalit people to use public wells to draw water for their homes. Often, Dalit women were not permitted to approach public wells for fear that they would "pollute" the water for upper-caste people. Ambedkar began an agitation to

Figure 4.3. Dr. Bhimrao Ambedkar. Source: Wikimedia Commons, https://commons.wikimedia.org/wiki/File:Dr._Bhimrao_Ambedkar.jpg.

make it illegal to discriminate at wells. He also argued that temples should be open for all people to visit and began huge public demonstrations to allow Dalits to enter these sacred sites. Significantly, Ambedkar strongly supported the codification of separate electorates for Dalits in Indian elections, along the same lines as separate electorates for Muslims, asserting that for lower-caste and Dalit people to gain legal and civil freedom, they needed representatives in all levels of government chosen by the Dalit populations themselves.

In 1932, the British proposed a series of separate electorates for depressed classes, another name for Dalits. Gandhi, on hearing this news, threatened to fast until he died unless it was overturned because of his fear that separate electorates for Dalits would be divisive in the larger Congress political movement and undermine Indian unity. Afraid of the possible Congress Party pushback that Dalits would endure if Gandhi died, Ambedkar was forced to give in and accept reserved seats for Dalits rather than separate electorates, but this concession soured the two movements' working relationship.[10] Ambedkar, and many in his political movement, felt that Congress did not speak for Dalits or have their best interests in mind.

The 1920s and early 1930s were also a turning point in Indian women's organizing for political power and civil rights. By the 1920s, reforming the status of women had been an important topic of Indian nationalism for decades, often with an emphasis on single issues like violence against women, purdah (the veiling and seclusion of women), women's and girls' illiteracy, or the pressure for widows to burn themselves alive on the funeral pyres of their husbands.[11] In the 1920s, Indian women began organizing on a national scale to define Indian women's needs and rights and to make changes in their own communities. In the early part of the twentieth century, several regional women's clubs and societies began forming and were often associated with religious reform organizations or political associations. In 1918, one of the first national women's rights advocacy organizations, the Women's Indian Association (WIA), was organized. The WIA initially focused on issues of health and welfare for women, with specific campaigns to prohibit prostitution and temple dancing, but soon after its founding, it branched out to discussions of purdah, women's literacy, suffrage, and, significantly, Indian nationalism. The WIA published a journal, *Stri Dharma* (The Sphere of Women) that allowed women to connect with each other and extend the mission of the association.[12] Other women's organizations grew out of international organizations, like the YWCA and the National Commission of Women: India, and these groups kept Indian women connected with the large international women's movement advocating for universal suffrage and international equality. In 1927, the WIA helped to form the All-India Women's Conference, a rights organization that would have an even larger reach and that brought women into national politics in meaningful ways.

One of the most important moves these nationally organized women's political movements took was to position women as a political constituency in need of both welfare and political responsibility. Male and female rights advocates created social work clinics that nursed women and children, supported schools, and opened hospitals and women's homes. They also advocated for the inclusion of women in legislatures, police forces, and the judiciary and fought for legal changes that would make it more possible for women to safely engage in society in general. By actively trying to change Indian society, women's rights activists argued that women qualified themselves for full citizenship in the Indian state.

## ORGANIZING FOR INDIAN NATIONHOOD

In a 1930 letter to his daughter from prison, Jawaharlal Nehru, a Congress leader and the future first prime minister of India, wrote "In India today, we are making history."[13] The political organizing of the 1920s laid a foundation for a serious push for Indian independence in the 1930s and 1940s. In late 1929, the Indian National

Figure 4.4. Gandhi on his way to Dandi during the Salt March. Source: Wikimedia Commons, https://commons.wikimedia.org/wiki/Category:Salt_March?uselang=fr#/media/File:Marche_sel.jpg.

Congress declared that its intention was to work for *purna swaraj,* or complete independence, from Great Britain.[14] Congress members chose a mobilization against the salt tax as their first campaign for purna swaraj. The salt tax laws burdened Indians with additional high costs for salt purchases and prohibited Indians from manufacturing their own salt. The salt tax laws, in addition to bringing in significant revenue for the British, disproportionately hurt the poorest Indians because salt was necessary for all home cooking. The Congress and Gandhi proposed a large-scale, national operation that would emphasize the way British imperialism directly and negatively impacted everyday life in India.[15] In March and April of 1930, Gandhi marched 240 miles over twenty-four days from Sabarmati Ashram to Dandi, a town on India's west coast, and made salt on the beach. The march stopped in every town, allowing Gandhi to bring the message of independence throughout the country. More than 250,000 Indians participated in some part of the march, and more than sixty thousand people were arrested for salt manufacture, including much of the Congress leadership. The Salt March created significant support for independence among a broad swath of the Indian population and built a broader sense of India as a single country.

During the 1920s and 1930s, the Muslim League also supported an Indian nationalism that would allow them to represent the needs of Indian Muslims on terms of equality with Hindus. The league saw Congress as primarily an organization representing Hindu Indians.[16] Members of the All-India Muslim

League felt that within Congress politics, the concerns of Muslims and other minorities were treated as secondary to the goal of independence, and they began working to articulate new visions of Indian independence and unity. In his 1930 presidential address, Mohammad Iqbal, a poet, professor, and Muslim leader, argued that India needed to be thought of as a federation, with many different and largely autonomous nations within its larger structure and at least one Indian state as a homeland for Indian Muslims. With this idea in mind, the All-India Muslim League characterized their fight as twofold: fighting for India's federal independence and struggling to be seen by all Indians as an equal partner to Congress in the building of a coherent nationwide federation.[17]

Throughout the 1930s, the relationship between Congress and the Muslim League became more and more strained. Congress consistently refused to grapple with the idea that they were the representatives of some, but not all, constituencies in India. The Congress argued that religion-based or caste-based politics, like that of the Muslim League or Dalit organizing, were dangerous for the nation, confirmed all British arguments about Indians being unable to live together peacefully, and undermined the nationalist movement. But leaders of the Muslim League, like Iqbal and Muhammad Jinnah, contended that Congress was unwilling to partner with minority organizations and did not take their requests seriously. It is certainly true that Indian Muslims have never been a single entity with the same needs or political preferences. Many Indian Muslims were uncomfortable with the claim by the Muslim League that the league should be the sole voice of Muslim interests in India.[18] Still, the Muslim League held considerable sway with many politically active Muslim communities and was a powerful advocate of Indian Muslim political interests. Congress's dismissal of the Muslim League's claims to speak on behalf of Indian Muslims as a legitimate separate entity further alienated the Congress and the league. The dismissal fostered more aggressive claims to nationhood for Indian Muslims and, ultimately, the rationale for partition.

The organizing and protests of the early 1930s began to be channeled differently after the enactment of the 1935 British Government of India Act that included an entirely rewritten Indian constitution that offered Indian people a little more autonomy. The act strengthened provincial legislatures and put them under the control of Indians but with a British governor in place. It also created built-in seats for Indians in the central legislature and on executive councils and reserved some seats for Muslims and Dalits in provincial and central legislatures. Supporters of the new policies were trying to placate some of the longest-standing grievances of the nationalist movement by making it easier for Indians to enter the Indian civil service and allowing Indians to hold higher-ranking positions in the army. Although the reforms offered significant new power to Indians in the government, it was too late for the British government of India to subdue the nationalists. The 1935 act enabled the Congress to transition from a mass movement into a political party and provided for 1937 provincial elections. Congress members successfully contested over half of the 1,500 seats in these elections and formed governments in seven provinces, including Bombay and the UP. Victorious Congress candidates, for a combination of reasons, were insensitive to working hard to cultivate Muslim support; it must be noted that throughout India, the Muslim League received less than 5 percent of the total Muslim vote.

In the 1940s, protests opposing India's involvement in World War II, and calls for the British to quit India, emerged after over two decades of continually more intense questioning of the British colonial system in India.

# 5

## INDEPENDENCE, PARTITION, AND A NEW INDIAN STATE

### WORLD WAR II AND INDEPENDENCE

In the years between 1939 and 1942, several events profoundly changed the future of Indian nationalism and the Indian state. In September 1939, without consulting Indian politicians and lawmakers, the British Raj declared that India would enter World War II along with the rest of the British Empire.[1] The political sentiment of Gandhi and the Indian National Congress was generally against India joining the war. Still, so many Indian soldiers were part of the forces fighting Nazi Germany, Japan, Italy, and associated nations that the Indian contingent constituted one of the largest military forces in the conflict. Over two and a half million Indian soldiers fought in the war, and more than eighty-seven thousand died.[2]

At home, India's entrance into World War II led to significant British crackdowns on freedom of speech and assembly. The British Raj reinstated and strengthened many emergency laws in the name of war morale and used these new laws to clamp down on rising nationalist dissatisfaction with continued colonial rule.[3] While increased censorship is not uncommon in wartime, emergency provisions were significantly stricter on Indian media and politics than they were in Britain. Throughout the war, British censors seized Indian newspaper presses, banned books, imprisoned Indian nationalists, and rerouted cloth and food grain supplies to British and American army depots stationed in India.

Gandhi and other Congress leaders resorted to authoring anti-war pleas and letters to political leaders. Other Indians embraced the maxim, "The enemy of my enemy is my friend." Subhas Chandra Bose, a former Congress Party leader, escaped house arrest in 1942 and flew to Germany, where he urged Indians to join the Indian National Army (INA) and fight British colonialism by taking the sides of Nazi Germany and imperial Japan. Approximately forty thousand Indians

Figure 5.1. Indian troops arriving on an Allied base in Singapore in 1941. Indian forces were active in both the European and Pacific fronts. Source: Wikimedia Commons, https://commons.wikimedia.org/wiki/ File:Newly-arrived_Indian_troops.jpg.

enlisted in the INA. Although it was not an influential fighting force, they would play a role in the aftermath of the war in ending British colonialism.[4]

Indian negative public opinion of the British Raj from 1941 to 1943 heightened as Bengal and much of Eastern India began to experience the effects of a terrible famine. Food shortages caused by violent weather, crop disease, and the British Empire's loss of control over areas of Burma to the Japanese were exacerbated by the Raj's demands that foodstuffs be distributed to British, American, and Indian soldiers first. At the same time, the British Raj's unwillingness to crack down on Bengali war and famine profiteers, including land grabbers, drove the price of staples like rice, pulses, and cloth unmanageably high, while staple foods and cloth moldered in British silos. More than three million people starved to death during the famine years. Although controversy exists over some of the specific causes of the famine, Nobel Prize-winning economist Amartya Sen has asserted that the famine was manmade rather than environmental and that British government policies were primarily responsible for the extreme loss of life during the famine.[5]

Despite the British wartime attempts to stifle Indian nationalist sentiments in public, Indian anti-colonial activists of all stripes began to believe that the end of the war could also herald the end of colonial rule in India. As a result, many Indian political activists used the war years to begin activities positioning themselves for the impending new era. Women's rights activists began agitating for universal suffrage and equal rights. Dalit organizers reemphasized the need for separate electorates for Dalits. Muslim League politicians, meanwhile, began to advocate for the creation of a separate Indian Muslim nation rather than remaining a minority in India.

In March 1940, the All-India Muslim League clarified their position on colonial rule, Indian independence, and the governing of Indian Muslim-majority provinces, asserting, "[Muslims] are a nation according to any definition of a nation, and they must have their homelands, their territory, and their state."[6] The league passed the 1940 Lahore Resolution demanding that Muslim-majority states should be consolidated to create "autonomous and sovereign states."[7] Although this resolution was not necessarily a call for the creation of Pakistan, as the South Asian Muslim state would later be called, it represented a first step toward the partitioning of the Indian subcontinent into an Indian state and a Pakistani state in 1947. As early as 1931, the possibility of this state had been discussed as a Muslim homeland in South Asia but never embraced as a real political solution.[8] The Lahore Resolution allowed Jinnah and the Muslim League to refer to Indian Muslims as a majority constituency and to make demands for more representation and power. After the Lahore Resolution, relations between the Muslim League and the Congress, already strained to a breaking point, became functionally defunct.

In August 1942, despite extensive censorship and political intimidation by the British Raj's wartime emergency laws, the INC declared a final and decisive program called the Quit India Movement, demanding that the British leave India once and for all. Gandhi contended in his speech announcing the new movement, "The mantra is Do or Die. We should either free India or die in the attempt; we shall not live to see the perpetuation of our slavery."[9] Gandhi urged journalists, government officials, princes, soldiers, students, and educators to pledge their allegiance to Congress and the Indian people to fight together to rid India of British rule. The declaration of the Quit India Movement coincided with the British Raj's declaration that the INC was an illegal terrorist organization. The British Raj arrested most of the Congress leadership shortly after Gandhi's Quit India speech. The Congress leadership remained imprisoned for at least two years. During that time, movement leaders continued to write and publish, helping to fuel an overwhelming call for Indian independence. Holding Indian political prisoners during the war, and especially the imprisonment of popular figures like Jawaharlal Nehru and Mahatma Gandhi, helped to turn the tide of popular opinion in India firmly against the British Raj.

Figure 5.2. Quit India procession in Bangalore, 1942. Thousands of Indians protested British colonialism in India. Source: Wikimedia Commons, https://commons.wikimedia.org/wiki/File:QUITIN2.JPG.

## CONSTITUTING A NEW NATION

By war's end, the British had freed the Congress political prisoners. The British called elections for an Indian Constituent Assembly to begin drafting an Indian constitution. Although the Constituent Assembly had representatives who were explicitly meant to represent minority communities, including a women's representative and two representatives of the "scheduled castes" (also known as Dalits), Congress dominated the assembly, leaving minority political organizations—particularly many Muslims, women, and Dalits—to feel underrepresented. The Dalit leader, B. R. Ambedkar, pointed out that rules requiring an assembly member to be associated with a larger political party to register to speak on the floor made it difficult for minority members to be heard.[10] The author of an article in *Roshni*, the journal of the All-India Women's Conference, bitterly charged that assembly congressmen tended to think of women's politics as frivolous and were not willing to have women's issues raised.[11] Jinnah himself, frustrated with his inability to get any traction on the discussion of Pakistan, called Congress not just a majority but a "brute majority" because of their unwillingness to engage with minority political organizations.[12]

In 1946, Jinnah, finding it difficult to negotiate with either Congress or the British Raj about the contours of a future Pakistan, in terms of powers, land, and its relationship to India, pushed for Muslims throughout India to go on strike. Jinnah called for a Direct Action Day on August 16, 1946, and urged Muslims throughout India to close shops, skip work, and protest for Pakistan. Although the strikes and marches were meant to be peaceful, the forcefulness of the call for action and the already high tempers meant that the large protests turned violent. There is no clear evidence of how the violence began, but within a few hours, the protest had turned into widespread rioting with violence by Muslim protestors and Hindu counter-protestors, with very little intervention on the part of the police to stop it. The Great Calcutta Killings, the week of rioting that followed Direct Action Day, left more than four thousand people dead and many more impacted by the chaos. The violence also spread widely, especially in the neighboring province of Bihar, where more than seven thousand people, mostly Muslims, were killed.[13] The event prompted increased tension between Muslim and Hindu communities across India. Only Gandhi's tour of the affected areas in Bihar eased tensions. Finally, after more than a week of violence and threats of more violence, Bihar returned to a very uneasy truce.

Events during Direct Action Day and the subsequent week of communal violence did lead the British to adopt a policy change, declaring that they would partition India to create two independent countries on the basis of majority religious population. The British government of India had drawn maps demarcating majority Hindu and Muslim provinces and population centers. Majority Hindu provinces would form India, and where majority Muslim areas could be consolidated on either side of India, Pakistan would be established. On June 3, 1947, it was announced that India and Pakistan would be partitioned and become independent on August 15 of the same year. The British urged rulers of princely states throughout the Indian subcontinent to choose either to join with Pakistan or India, ideally before independence and partition.

Such a restricted time frame for essentially three massive and complicated events—the British withdrawal from India (and Pakistan), Indian independence, and Pakistani independence—left little time for any policymakers to adequately organize a peaceful transfer of power. Undivided India had a large and relatively well-organized bureaucracy, but the nascent Pakistan government did not even have stationary or pens, let alone government buildings, treasuries, or state records. Virtually every tangible and human asset the Indian government owned needed to be divided, from books in state libraries, office supplies, and broadcasting equipment to allocations of government public servants and army officers.[14] None of these negotiations were clear-cut or easy, but many had serious ramifications that are still felt today. Significantly, the reorganization of the undivided Indian army and Indian security forces, and the shifting of army and police personnel to new posts while the partition took place in conjunction with an immediate draw down of the British army and security personnel, meant few military or security personnel could effectively disrupt partition-related violence and rioting. The most impossible job of all was protecting the migrants shifting across newly delineated and poorly understood borders.

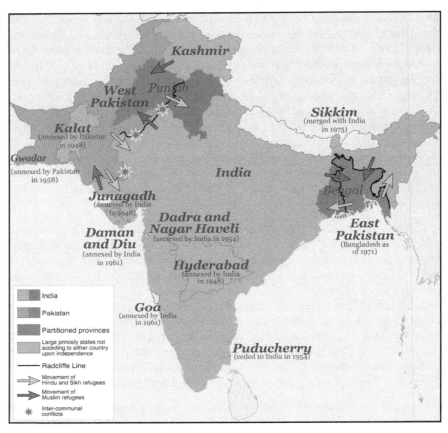

Map 5.1. Map of the partition of India into India and Pakistan. Source: Wikimedia Commons, https://commons.wikimedia.org/wiki/File: Partition_of_India_1947_en.svg.

## PARTITION

The partition of India was, first and foremost, the splitting of India into India and Pakistan based upon religious-majority provinces. London policymakers selected Cyril Radcliffe, a British lawyer who had never been to India before and who had no specialized knowledge of the subcontinent's geography, to draw the final boundary lines. While the British had maps showing locations of Hindu- and Muslim-majority provinces, especially around the proposed borders, Hindu and Muslim communities lived packed next to each other, and disentangling centuries of cultural community was more complicated than drawing a simple line. Moreover, the British did not announce the final boundary lines until August 17, two days after Indian independence and three days after Pakistani independence. People who lived near the proposed border were uncertain as to whether they were in Pakistan or India, which added to mounting chaos.

The days and weeks before independence—set to begin August 14, 1947, for Pakistan and August 15, 1947, for India—were marked by increasing communal violence, especially in areas near the assumed borders in Punjab and Bengal. Uncertain of whether they would be safe, separate populations of faith-based populations in each of the new countries began making and executing plans to go either to India—for the Hindu and Sikh populations—or Pakistan—for the Muslim populations. The partition of the Indian subcontinent was one of the largest mass migration events in world history, with more than fifteen million people crossing the borders between 1947 and 1951.[15]

Some refugees planned to return to their homes after the violence and confusion had died down, while others, feeling concerned for their ongoing safety, planned to migrate permanently. Many people risked a hasty crossing, fleeing from deadly communal violence with little more than the clothes on their backs and merging with columns of other migrants that were easy targets for violent agitators. Estimates are that more than one million people were killed in partition violence, with the carnage affecting Muslims, Hindus, and Sikhs in similar numbers.[16] Women were special targets of partition violence; in addition to women and girls who were killed, at least one million women were raped and abducted. In the days and weeks leading up to formal independence and partition, Gandhi, Nehru, Jinnah, and other prominent national figures all pled for an end to the violence, professing themselves committed to minority rights and begging for

Figure 5.3. Special trains ran from India to Pakistan and from Pakistan to India, transporting refugees. Source: Wikimedia Commons, https://commons.wikimedia.org/wiki/File:A_refugee_special_train_at_Ambala_Station_during_partition_of_India.jpg.

an end to retaliatory violence, but people were scared, confused, and angry about the extreme violence committed against their families and communities and often resorted to mob-like violence.

## INDEPENDENCE

The independence days, August 14 for Pakistan and August 15 for India, were marked by celebrations. Nehru called India's Independence Day a "tryst with destiny," while Jinnah laid out his hopes for a Pakistan that would be free of communal fighting.[17] Despite the formal recognition of national liberation, the first independence days were marked by the ongoing violence of partition and the chaotic immigration of millions of refugees. Especially in Delhi and other Indian cities with large Muslim populations, mobs of Hindu rioters drove thousands of Muslims from their homes and into makeshift camps but not out of the city, leading to a large number of internally displaced people on top of the refugees coming into the cities.[18] Finding a way to resettle all of these displaced people strained both new countries, and these newborn nations did not have sufficient resources to help resettle all their refugees. Numerous small farmer refugees did not have the capital to purchase new lands in India or Pakistan and were rendered landless laborers.

Other partition-related problems fostered widespread distrust among various groups. The new Indian government treated Indian Muslims—most who had nothing to do with the violence around partition or who had been victims of it— like potential traitors. Muslims in government were forced to sign loyalty pledges, and many Muslims outside of government were unceremoniously fired from their jobs.[19] In early 1948, during the immediate aftermath of the violence, Gandhi took what would become his last major stand in the name of minority rights. He undertook a six-day hunger strike to highlight the plight of minorities in India. Although his hunger strike was only partly successful, it did encourage Indian politicians to focus on the problem of minority rights in the newly independent nation. Gandhi's hunger strike, combined with his assassination shortly afterward— on January 30, 1948, by Hindu nationalist party loyalist Nathuram Godse because of the Mahatma's support for Muslim rights—incentivized framers of the Indian constitution to build some protections for minorities.

Postindependence India retained at first, and continues to retain, several legacies of British colonial rule. In part because of the country's large number of languages, and in part because the educated elite had gone to schools taught in English, the English language was a de facto, if not official, national language. Indeed, in 1948, legislators from Southern India revolted at attempts to make Hindi the language of government and public discourse. To this day, the most sought-after schools and universities in India are taught in English, and many people speak English fluently. Similarly, the members of the Indian Constitution Committee used the 1935 constitution as a model for India's postindependence government, meaning that much of the underpinning of Indian law and justice has been influenced heavily by English common law and colonial governments. India's foreign relationships, both directly after independence and now, have heavily featured former and current members of the British commonwealth, and Great Britain and India continue to have a robust economic relationship.[20] Despite these lingering colonial influences, at independence, the Indian public were keen to assert themselves as their own country. As India turned toward independence, the next steps for the constitution committee involved writing and implementing the new constitution. Yet the continued bad blood with Pakistan, as well as uncertainty at its own borders, made India's first two independent decades uneasy ones.

# 6

## REORGANIZATION AND RECONSTRUCTION OF INDIAN LIFE, 1950–1965

### INDIA'S CONSTITUTION

Although India became an independent state on August 15, 1947, there was still significant work to be done to define the rules, contours, and politics of the new state. Most importantly, there was the drafting of governing documents. Although the Constituent Assembly, which had been negotiated between the British and nationalist leaders, had been elected in 1946 and had been working since then, much of their pre-independence work related to defining the scope of the independent Indian nation. When partition was announced, the Constituent Assembly began organizing and managing partition and independence. After independence, Jawaharlal Nehru was appointed prime minister, and the Constituent Assembly took on a dual role as a federal governing body and the authors of a constitution. Dr. B. R. Ambedkar, the well-known Dalit activist and legal scholar, was India's first law minister and the main architect of the Indian constitution.

For Ambedkar and the constitution committee, many questions needed to be addressed in the document. What were the governing principles of the newly independent India? How should the nation be organized? What guidelines were needed to integrate principles and structure? Similar debates raged over how Indian states should be organized. Should the country keep the colonial governing boundary lines or draw new ones? The constitution established a federal system, with power divided between the national and state governments, but what powers should be delegated to the federal government and what powers should be delegated to the states? What freedoms should be included in the fundamental freedoms section? Did freedom of speech clash with freedom of religion? Who were minorities in India? Should the lower castes and Dalits be considered minorities for

Figure 6.1. Dignitaries at the first Republic Day parade in 1950, including B. R. Ambedkar, the drafter of the constitution. Source: Wikimedia Commons, https://commons.wikimedia.org/wiki/File:Dr._B._R._Ambedkar_among_other_dignitaries_at_India%27s_first_Republic_Day_parade_(7th_from_right).jpg.

the purpose of state protections? What about women? Religious minorities? None of these questions had easy answers, and debates about each of them were fierce in the Constituent Assembly. The draft constitution was completed in late 1949 and ratified on January 26, 1950. The date, designated Republic Day, is still celebrated as a holiday in India of equal, if not greater, importance than Independence Day.

As ratified, the constitution drew heavily on pre-independence and British governing documents, including the 1928 Nehru Report and the 1935 Government of India Act. Although many leaders from Southern India, where the most common languages spoken are quite different from Hindi and other languages spoken in the north, asserted that states be reorganized based on the majority language spoken in the region; Nehru and many Congress stalwarts felt that linguistic states would undermine ideas of Indian unity. For this reason, state boundaries were initially roughly mapped onto British provincial boundaries. Many states in North India, like Orissa and Bengal, were organized along linguistic lines, but this was not the case with most Indian states, particularly those in South India, which caused friction for the young country.

The framers of the constitution established a bicameral legislature (two separate legislative bodies) that was similar to the British House of Commons and House of Lords—the Lok Sabha (People's Assembly) and the Rajya Sabha (Lords' Assembly). The founding document also included provisions for a strong independent judiciary and a federal high court. The constitution banned the caste system and included several provisions to define and protect minorities, particularly lower castes and religious minorities. The constitution attempted to ensure that government positions, educational opportunities, and legislative representation were available to these previously marginalized groups. It also included provisions for a robust freedom of speech and freedom of religion.[1]

The constitution also instituted universal adult suffrage, giving all people, including women, the poor, and the landless, the opportunity to vote. In a country, which in 1950 had more than four hundred million people who spoke more than one hundred different languages, and a literacy rate of less than 20 percent, government workers found universal suffrage a difficult problem to solve.[2] Huge investments of both time and money went into expanding the eligible voter rolls and informing people of their rights to vote. Ballots were prepared in several languages, and the government instituted a system of image-based voting to help illiterate adults decipher the ballot. Political parties and politicians were depicted in simple, well-advertised pictures.[3] Indian ballots still include pictures of party symbols despite a very significant rise in literacy rates among all parts of the population over the last seven decades.

Figure 6.2. A woman coming to vote in New Delhi, 1952. The pictures on the wall (bicycle, camel, cow and calf, etc.) are the lists of the candidates with their party affiliation. Source: Wikimedia Commons, https://commons.wikimedia.org/wiki/File:A_refugee_woman_being_given_her_ballot_papers,_at_a_polling_station_in_Lajpat_Nagar,_1952.jpg.

Ambedkar, in his speech to the Constituent Assembly after the constitution was approved, urged Indians to recognize the work that would need to go into protecting, supporting, and upholding the promise of the Indian constitution. He urged that Indian democracy was fragile and would need to be supported not just through government dictates but with social and economic changes that recognized the inequalities of Indian society in the forms of caste and class oppression, and marginalization.

## ORGANIZING AND REORGANIZING THE INDIAN STATE AND SOCIETY

Although lawmakers, including Nehru and Ambedkar, used many of the bureaucratic ideas of the British Raj as a road map for the initial organization of independent India, there were some things that needed to change. Economically, Nehru and others argued that India needed to reorient the state away from colonial systems of extraction and economic degradation and toward Indian self-sufficiency. Similarly, policies of land taxes and excessive duties to landlords needed to be rethought to allow for the improvement of the lives of small farmers. The women's movement was also working to make sure women's rights remained at the forefront of legislative concerns and social protests.

From before independence, Indian economists suggested the country implement economic planning to define priorities among several pressing needs. After independence, a planning commission was established to create the first five-year plan, which was adopted and begun in 1951.[4] The 1951 plan focused on government-directed nationalized industry, making health care more accessible across the country, building national industrial and technical education, and creating a more self-sufficient Indian economy. The national government regulated imports, promoted Indian-made items, and limited foreign investment and ownership in Indian companies. The planning commission hoped that investments in education, health, and Indian industry would bring more Indians into better-paying jobs and break cycles of agrarian and urban poverty. These five-year plans continued until 2017, each focusing on different issues of social, political, and economic growth.

Planning and government control were conceived as paths to a more equitable democracy, and the plans emphasized building equality and a strong Indian nation. Still, the plans sometimes stifled social and economic growth. Government officials, sometimes called the License and Permit Raj, collectively created what often felt like a nanny state, requiring that even the smallest ventures be highly regulated and rejecting foreign investment in India. The promotion of Indian-made goods and industries also meant that consumer goods like clothing, household goods, and automobiles were often less available in India than in other parts of the world.

A major key in rethinking Indian society and the national economy was to dismantle the system of agrarian and village life that privileged landlords and village headmen over tenants and small farmers. After independence, several interrelated bills sought to do just that through land reform. Customary rules requiring a certain number of hours of work on a landlord's property by renters were banned, caps on the number of acres any individual landowner could hold were instituted, the rate of allowable rents was reduced, and tenancy rights were legislated. The central government also supported a series of cooperative unions to give small farmers better access to seeds, fertilizers, and livestock, and to allow stronger bargaining power when selling farm materials. Villages were also required to organize village councils to govern villages, with mandatory requirements to include a woman.[5] Although the policies seemed to be laudatory and specific in written form, they were often overlooked and under-enforced. Many of them were overturned after legal challenges from landowners, making them more ineffectual than many Indians considered desirable.

India successfully drafted and ratified a constitution that laid the groundwork for a mostly stable government structure, but even before it was ratified, many, if not most, politicians and activists understood that it would need to be amended. Before the Indian constitution was ten years old, there were at least ten amendments.[6] Some were substantial and controversial, like the rewriting of the fundamental freedoms section to limit freedom of speech that could be dangerous or damaging to India. Prime Minister Jawaharlal Nehru worked for the first amendment to the constitution after unsuccessfully attempting to regulate newspaper publications that the government felt were attempting to incite social violence. Other changes were made to accommodate important social and economic needs, such as the eighth amendment, which extended the reserved seats for scheduled castes—otherwise known as Dalits—in the central and state legislatures. Still more changes were made to acknowledge the perceived shortcomings in India's state structures, in light of subsequent events, such as the amendments that changed India's borderline with Pakistan after the conclusion of negotiations.

One of the bigger shifts was on the issue of state reorganization. Although the Indian government initially rejected new linguistic states, regional leaders argued that states' boundaries should be drawn around the primary language spoken in the region. In 1952, Potti Sriramulu, a former Gandhian freedom fighter, began a fast to the death to draw attention to the need for a separate Telugu-speaking state. Nehru and other leaders were initially unwilling to consider new linguistic states, but Sriramulu's fast promoted widespread agitations for a separate state. In January 1953, Nehru agreed to a separate linguistic state for Telugu speakers, Andhra Pradesh, but not before Sriramulu died from his fast. The success of the Andhra protests prompted renewed calls to reorganize Indian states along linguistic and cultural lines. In 1953, Nehru appointed the States Reorganization Commission, which was tasked with rethinking the Indian map. The commission completed its work in 1956, largely organizing Indian states linguistically. Since then, Indian

Map 6.1. Map of Indian states and territories and their primary languages.
Source: Wikimedia Commons, https://commons.wikimedia.org/wiki/
File:Official_language_map_of_India_by_state_and_union_territory_(claimed_
and_disputed_hatched).svg.

states and territories have been reorganized regularly, with the newest state added
in 2014 (Telangana) and the newest territory in 2019 (Ladakh).[7]

Activists working for minority groups also tried to make significant changes
to the Indian governing documents and society to better place their constituency
in the new nation. In the first elections after independence, Dalit political leaders,
including Ambedkar, noted that reserved seats for scheduled castes (generally Dalit
castes) without separate electorates meant that the Dalit community was likely to
be represented by parties for whom Dalit issues were secondary at best. Similarly,
many Dalit leaders began agitating for economic and social reforms guaranteeing

that the protections promised in the constitution would be honored in society. In 1957, the Republican Party was founded. It was devoted to the establishment of a social democracy, and to recognizing and changing systematic oppression against the lower castes, Dalits, and poor Indians. Although the party was small, and though it fractured often, it was an important site for Dalit politics in the 1960s. Other Dalit leaders, like Jagjivan Ram of the Congress Party, continued to advocate for Dalit issues outside of specifically Dalit-based political organizations.

Women's advocacy organizations saw the general move toward equality after independence as an opportunity to make some legal and social strides to ensure women were included in the new Indian state. In addition to the inclusion of women in village government, women's organizations successfully challenged laws forcing women to resign from jobs in both the public and private sectors after marriage. Similarly, women pushed for labor unions to include women's work, and when this proved difficult, they created their own unions. But all was not smooth for women's rights activists. Changing rules for marriage, divorce, inheritance, and other civil regulations and statutes to make them fairer and more universal to all women had long been a priority of women's rights groups. Some changes were made to the Hindu civil code in the 1950s, modifying rules allowing women to inherit property from their birth families, but sweeping changes concerning divorce and alimony, the banning of marital rape, and other equality-focused measures were not adopted. Moreover, moves to try to remove religious affiliations from civil law were roundly rejected, leaving independent India with the same religiously based civil law codes that were in practice during British rule. Even today, marriages, divorces, child custody, and inheritance are all based on an applicant's religious affiliation, despite many attempts to change this legal regulation.

## UNDERSTANDING INDIA'S BORDERS: HYDERABAD AND KASHMIR

At independence, there were more than five hundred kingdoms and princely states in India, and all of them needed to choose to become part of Pakistan, India, or to remain independent. One pressing problem for both India and Pakistan upon independence was how to integrate the kingdoms and princely states into the newly formed nation-states. By 1950, almost all princely states had chosen India or Pakistan, largely based on geography, and virtually all of them were integrated into the country either as part of neighboring states or provinces or as their own state or province within the country. There were two princely states that posed significant problems: Hyderabad and Kashmir.

Hyderabad and Kashmir were both large and prosperous principalities, and at independence, the rulers of both states hoped to remain independent. Hyderabad and Kashmir had several other similarities. Both had rulers who practiced a different religion than most of their subjects. Hyderabad had a ruler—the nizam— who was Muslim, while the population of Hyderabad State was majority Hindu. Kashmir was the opposite; the ruler—the raja—was Hindu, while the population was majority Muslim. Both were wealthy, important states in British India. Both principalities had a high degree of income inequality and unrest among elites, commoners, and peasants.

The geography of the two states, while quite different in relationship to India and Pakistan, also made the idea of Hyderabadi or Kashmiri independence difficult. Hyderabad State was directly in the middle of the Indian subcontinent, and if it had been allowed to be an independent country, it would have been entirely enclosed by India, an outcome that India government officials hated. Hyderabad contained rich agricultural lands and was, even then, known for its technology. Although Kashmir was on an outside border of both India and Pakistan—and therefore could go either way geographically—both Indian and Pakistani government officials and military officers understood Kashmir to be a strategic borderland between India, Pakistan, and China. Kashmir was also the home of Jawaharlal Nehru, India's first prime minister, and an important summer capital for the Indian government.

In Hyderabad, the nizam, a strong supporter of the Muslim League, initially planned to join Pakistan. In 1947, realizing the choice was impossible given the geography of the two countries, he opted to sign an agreement with India that Hyderabad would pursue independence while not permanently ruling out joining India. The princely state of Hyderabad was also experiencing internal strife. Conflicts in the poorest part of Hyderabad—between a coalition of communists and peasants demanding more access to land and higher prices for agrarian goods, and Hyderabadi officials demanding higher taxes—intensified the violence. In September 1948, the Indian government used the internal conflict as a rationale to militarily step into Hyderabad and intervene in the conflict. The Indian government classed the conflict as religiously motivated, with the nizam's Muslim soldiers harassing Hindu peasants, but both sides in the internal Hyderabadi conflict agreed that the fight was about taxes and land. By classing the conflict as religious, the Indian government ignored the complaints about land rights, taxes, and the prices of agrarian goods. India, allowing the conflict to continue, attained its end of capturing Hyderabad. Within four days, the nizam surrendered, and the Indian state installed a military governor and officially integrated Hyderabad into India.[8]

Although the Kashmiri situation had some similarities to Hyderabad, its differences meant that while the Hyderabad conflict came to a quick, if acrimonious, conclusion, the conflict around the state of Kashmir continues today, over seventy years later. The Indian and Pakistani governments both claimed Kashmir. The Kashmiri raja, Hari Singh, preferred to remain independent and attempted in 1947 to sign agreements with India and Pakistan that allowed more time to make a final choice. India refused to sign this agreement, but Pakistan, hoping to ultimately hold Kashmir, signed. In the meantime, much of the population, exhausted from the high taxes and minimal government support in Kashmir, saw Pakistan as a better option than independence. Kashmiri Muslims, especially around the border with Pakistan, began violent anti-state action supported by the Pakistani military. Hari Singh asked India to intervene in the military action with Pakistan, but Nehru refused to engage unless Kashmir agreed to formally join India. In October 1947, the situation for the Kashmiri raja was desperate, and he agreed to join India, with some clauses built into the agreement that would ensure some Kashmiri autonomy. In 1948, after the signing of the Kashmiri Accession Agreement, India engaged Pakistan in the first of four wars—the others being in 1965, 1971, and 1999. Kashmir was a concern in all four.[9]

## INDIA AND THE WORLD

Before Indian independence, India's formal relationship with the world was limited by its status as a colony. Indian nationalists interacted with other anti-colonial leaders around the world; British-controlled India had trading, political, and geographic relationships with other countries and empires; and India, even though it was now independent, chose to remain part of the British commonwealth, connecting it to other British-controlled colonies throughout the world. After independence, India had the freedom to forge new international relationships. Some relationships, particularly those with close commonwealth partners like Australia and South Africa, continued in relatively unchanged forms after independence. This was not the case with major or, in China's case, emerging powers. The need was particularly pressing because India gained independence at the beginning of the Cold War period. After World War II, the US and the USSR began solidifying their spheres of influence and allies in preparation for what would become a global struggle between two substantially different ideologies (communism and liberal democracy) that continued over four decades.

The US and USSR found newly independent states, like India, to be important opportunities to expand their influence. India, along with many other newly independent colonies, felt uncomfortable with solidifying a Cold War alliance and instead chose to be nonaligned. Indian national political leaders feared entering tight alliances with either of the two Cold War original superpowers would undermine their hard-won independence. Being nonaligned allowed India to work with all comers, including taking aid from all sides. Nehru and others argued that if all the former colonies and small countries could work together, they would be able to be a third force in an international system that was dominated by the US and USSR.[10]

Just as India's internal borders were not firmly settled upon independence, its external borders were also uncertain. In the first twenty years after independence, India fought three border wars—two in 1948 and 1965 with Pakistan about control of Kashmir, and one in 1962 with China. The Indo-Pak wars of 1948 and 1965 were largely focused on Kashmir and continued the anger and distrust stemming from partition and the struggle for independence. Both India and Pakistan felt that Kashmir was necessary to their survival, and both countries felt that they had the more compelling claim to the state. The United Nations negotiated a

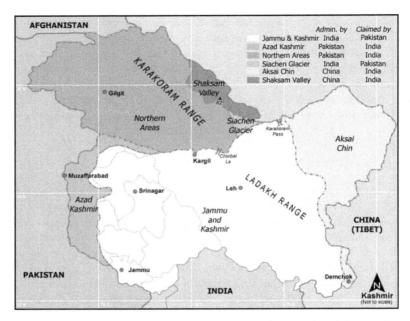

Map 6.2. Map of Kashmir, showing the Line of Control and disputed areas. Source: Wikimedia Commons, https://commons.wikimedia.org/wiki/File:Kashmir_2007.JPG.

ceasefire in early 1949, bringing an end to the fighting and setting up the Line of Control, which designated part of Kashmir as controlled by India and another part controlled by Pakistan. Neither India nor Pakistan complied with the other components of the ceasefire agreement. The agreement required Pakistani soldiers to evacuate Kashmir, which they did not do, and India agreed to hold a referendum on Kashmiri control, offering voters in Kashmir three options—join Pakistan, remain in India, or become independent—which it did not do. The second Indo-Pak war in 1965 lasted seventeen days and was fought on similar provocations, and the positions of Kashmir, India, and Pakistan were largely unchanged after it.

While India was dealing with uncertainty in its relationship with Pakistan, it was also managing a tenuous relationship with China, which borders India to the northeast. In the 1950s, Indian diplomats were keen to cultivate a strong relationship with China. In 1949, Mao Zedong and his Communist Party won the Chinese Civil War with the nationalists and created the modern People's Republic of China. India was one of the first nations to recognize the new People's Republic of China, and at first, it hoped China would be a potential partner and leader of the nonaligned movement. After an initial rejection of nonalignment early on in Mao's rule, China, for about five years, considered itself nonaligned. By the late 1950s however, Mao's government shifted alignment to a promotion of worldwide communism, souring its relationships with many nonaligned countries, including India.

But perhaps more importantly than ideological differences, Indo-China tensions related directly to power politics and borders. India and China had never formally negotiated their border, instead falling back on borders the British and Tibetan governments constructed in the 1910s. China, in an attempt to consolidate control over Tibet, began encroaching on the "accepted" borderline in the 1950s, building new roads and military bases in what India thought of as Indian territory and backing up their encroachment with the publication of new maps showing a different borderline.[11] It did not help that India was open to welcoming into India what it considered to be refugees from Tibet, people who the Chinese considered to be dangerous provocateurs. In 1959, Tibet's Buddhist and political leader, the Dalai Lama, fled from Tibet to India. The Chinese feared that the Dalai Lama might set up a Tibetan government in exile in India. Throughout 1960 and 1961, India and China negotiated about these two issues, but no compromise was reached. In June 1962, skirmishes began in northeast India, with China pushing gradually further into Indian territory, and an undeclared war erupted. In October 1962, China unilaterally declared a ceasefire and retained the land they had won over the course of the war. There has never been an official resolution of the war.

The relative uncertainty and high level of change and conflict in the first few years of Indian independence speak both to the difficulty of creating a new, democratic state in general and to concerns of economic development, social change, and balancing a large, diverse population. Internally and externally, India was buffeted by uncertainty with their borders, their structure, and even their founding documents. These issues did not entirely go away as India settled into its place in the world.

# 7

## POLITICAL CHANGE, ENVIRONMENTAL CHANGE, 1966–1985

### FAMINE, GROW MORE FOOD, AND THE GREEN REVOLUTION

Throughout the nineteenth and twentieth centuries, famine and food insecurity plagued India. During the 1950s and 1960s, India experienced persistent food shortages, partly because of environmental factors—especially droughts—and partly because of demographic changes, including partition migration and population growth. India was forced, reluctantly, to annually accept food aid from the USSR and Western countries between 1949 and 1969, despite national leaders urging food self-sufficiency and instituting plans to increase Indian food yields. Grow More Food campaigns were instituted in the years just before independence and continued through the 1970s. The Ministry for Agriculture and Food Commissions urged more citizens to become cultivators and suggested changes to the Indian staple diet, away from wheat and rice and toward crops that were more drought-resistant, like groundnuts, yams, and tapioca. Women's groups, like the All-India Women's Conference, among others, urged Indians to skip one meal a week in the name of self-sufficiency. Nehru even floated the idea of allowing for serious food shortages rather than continuing to rely on food imports and aid.[1]

In the name of greater food security, the Indian government began a series of initiatives to remake domestic agriculture. The central and state governments suggested local-level farming changes such as village cooperatives, where peasants planned and sold their crops together, as well as food rationing and projects to increase the available farmland.[2] The Indian government began building large dams to try to remake arid wastelands into commercial farmland. These schemes were often done without environmental assessments, productivity plans, or consideration of the damage that the dams and collective farming would do to productive but small-scale farming communities. Generally, these projects did not measurably change India's ability to feed itself.[3]

Food aid to India from the West was often tied to economic development projects focused on building a more technological agrarian economy.[4] For example, US food aid was hindered by requirements to shift from diversified crop rotations to single-grain crops that would show greater yields but damage the soil, or the addition of fertilizer inputs that small farmers often could not afford. The Ministry of Agriculture had previously shied away from many of these more "modernized" farming techniques, in part because they required larger plots and more start-up funds than most Indian farmers possessed.

In May 1964, Jawaharlal Nehru died while still prime minister. India was in a fragile state politically and socially. Then the monsoon rains, which provide much of the water for farming across India, failed in 1965, 1966, and 1967, leaving much of India famine ridden. To stem village-level collapse, the government bought into the Green Revolution. This attention-getting project began in Mexico in the 1940s, when teams of scientists developed patented seeds that provided very high-yielding versions of staple crops, particularly wheat. Green Revolution farming relied on specific inputs of chemical fertilizers, irrigation, and pesticides during previously planned times in the growth cycle.[5] Inputs in the process had patents, so farmers needed to purchase new seeds, fertilizers, and pesticides at higher costs. In 1967, the Indian government began purchasing seeds—primarily wheat and rice—and fertilizers. The government then distributed them at a huge discount to farmers, especially farmers with larger landholdings. The amount of food produced went up by more than 20 percent and helped to stabilize food production in India for two decades, but it also created disadvantages for some farmers. The new style of farming favored larger farmers, as a result, small Dalit, lower-caste, and lower-class landholders and their families were often displaced. It also demanded monoculture, which was fine in good years, but in years where the crop failed, farms were devastated because of the lack of crop diversification.[6] Today, many scholars, policymakers, and farmers continue to be concerned about the level of farmer indebtedness, decreases in crop yields, and the longer-term ecological impact of Green Revolution-style agriculture, and they have begun to look for new ways to stabilize India's food production.[7]

## POLITICAL CHANGES AND POPULAR UPRISINGS

The death of Jawaharlal Nehru prompted a reshuffling of the leadership of the Congress Party that had run India since independence. Many important Congress Party members who would have been obvious successors to Nehru had died before him or were out of politics, and the new generation of leaders was still young. The party chose Lal Bahadur Shastri, a talented behind-the-scenes bureaucrat and party leader, as Nehru's successor. When Shastri also died in office two years after Nehru's death, the Congress Party and the government of India were at loose ends. Congress had been the only successful national party since independence, and the party was uncertain who would be best as a successor. After Shastri's death, the party appointed Nehru's daughter, Indira Gandhi, as head of the party, with

Figure 7.1. Indira Gandhi in 1961. Source: Wikimedia
Commons, https://upload.wikimedia.org/wikipedia/
commons/thumb/a/ad/Indira_Gandhi%2C_Paris_1961.tiff/
lossy-page1-4150px-Indira_Gandhi%2C_Paris_1961.tiff.jpg.

the idea that she would be little more than a puppet for party power brokers to use.[8] Instead, Gandhi proved to be a charismatic, astute, and ruthless politician with a strong anti-poverty agenda, and she was unwilling to bend to the more conservative members of the Congress Party. Indira Gandhi was also one of the first women in the world to lead a democratic country.

In the 1967 elections, regional political parties, especially those from Southern India, chipped away at the Congress Party majorities in the legislative body. Gandhi was forced to form a coalition government of socialist, communist, and left-leaning political parties, including some of the southern regional parties. The coalition granted a measure of power for Southern India and pushed out many moderate and conservative former Congress leaders. Gandhi styled herself as a friend to the poor and minorities with policies to support Dalits, women, and small farmers. Her first term was unremarkable, and it was primarily notable for her angering of moderate and conservative members of her own Congress Party. Her 1971 election slogan, "Get Rid of Poverty" ("*Garibi Hatao*"), increased her popularity among minorities, farmers, and the poor.[9]

In addition to being an unsettled time for the Congress Party, the late 1960s and early 1970s were a bad time for the Indian economy, marked by water, food, and cloth shortages across Northern India. The national government, attempting to support the agricultural sector, devalued the Indian rupee, causing prices for food and basic necessities to rise across the board. Economic turmoil fueled several important anti-government movements beginning in the mid-1960s in the Naxalbari region of West Bengal. Several years of poor crops meant many small farmers were forced to sell their land and to survive work as hired laborers or by renting land from larger property owners. Landlords in the region, desperate for cash themselves, raised rents so high that workers could never pay their rent based on the sale of their crop yields.

Additionally, many landlords in the region continued to demand illegal but customary free labor and sexual access to lower-caste and Dalit women tenants. Tenants, together with student activists from Calcutta, formed the Naxalbari Peasant Aid Committee to advocate for better leases, loan forgiveness, and increased reporting of tenant abuses to local police stations. In May 1967, a local landlord killed one of his tenants and bullied the local police to refuse to investigate. The Peasant Aid Committee, enraged by the failure of the government to investigate, began a campaign of violent protests, including burning all lease and loan records, harassing and killing local landlords, and ambushing police stations. The violence continued until the West Bengal state government, joined by the Communist Party, which had previously supported the peasants, cracked down on the protestors. Although many peasants were charged with violence, several leaders escaped and spread throughout the country. Similar Naxalite actions have taken hold in areas of high indebtedness or high poverty in the decades since. In the 1980s, a group of formally affiliated Naxalites, who are radical communists, founded the People's War Group in Andhra Pradesh. After being dismantled by the Andhra State police by the end of the 1990s, the movement shifted to Chhattisgarh and Jharkhand, where they set up military and administrative control over several extremely poor districts. In 2006, Manmohan Singh, who was then prime minister, labeled the Naxals one of the greatest threats to the Indian state. In recent years, the power of the movement seems to be waning.[10]

After the 1971 elections, many people had hopes that the central government would be more proactive in helping landless laborers, Dalits, and scheduled tribes. When changes were slow to materialize, several activists began protesting government inaction. Jayaprakash (J. P.) Narayan, a well-known freedom fighter from the nationalist movement and later leader of land reform movements, began to travel throughout India, urging people to join a civil disobedience action he called Total Revolution, which was similar to nationalist boycotts during the

1942 Quit India Movement. Narayan, dissatisfied with the central government's education policies, the economy, and land reform, called for a nonviolent overthrow of the government in favor of a people's swaraj (self-rule). The Total Revolution Movement was never a real threat to the Indian government, but it did resonate with those citizens who felt that independence had promised much but delivered little.

A related movement, the United Women's Anti-Price Rise Front, was also sparked by a feeling of helplessness in the face of rising prices and the perception of a corrupt government. Begun in Bombay by politically engaged women, the Anti-Price Rise Front protestors demonstrated against the large rise in government-set prices for food staples like onions, rice, and butter. Although previous political activists were movement leaders, the issues, particularly government-set food prices, brought out newcomers to politics, including poor and lower-caste women as well as middle-class housewives. Like the Total Revolution Movement, the United Women's Anti-Price Rise Front activists argued that the promise of an Indian nation that cared for and recognized its citizens was being smothered by government corruption and mismanagement.[11]

The 1970s also saw the recognition of other social justice works run by women. In 1979, Mother Teresa was awarded the Nobel Peace Prize for her founding of and work with the Order of the Missionaries of Charity, which she had run since 1950. Her work helping the poor was recognized globally through the expansion of her ministry to more than 123 countries worldwide. Although she was born an Albanian citizen, Mother Teresa spent her whole working life in India and became an Indian citizen in 1948. Under her direction, the Order of the Missionaries of Charity worked in the poorest areas of Calcutta, and later around the world, running orphanages, hospices, and nursing homes. Mother Teresa began her ministries in Calcutta at least in part due to the devastation she witnessed on a tour of Bengal during and just after the ravages of the Bengal famine of 1942.

Mother Teresa was not without controversy in India, especially for her staunch stances against divorce, contraception, and abortion, and the perception that her organization failed to offer adequate medical care, despite significant fundraising. In 1972, she was awarded the Jawaharlal Nehru Award for her work to promote international understanding. In 1980, she was awarded the highest Indian civilian honor, the Bharat Ratna. Mother Teresa died in 1997.[12]

Adivasi (indigenous) women were at the forefront of an environmental movement called the Chipko movement in Uttarakhand State, which is located in Northern India in the Himalayas. The women of the Chipko movement were frustrated by the government's ban on women collecting forest goods in their villages while simultaneously allowing private companies to clear-cut nearby forests. They fought for the protection of their forests and their ability to use them sustainably.

The early 1970s also saw the rise of the Akali Dal, a Sikh nationalist political party that argued for an autonomous Sikh region in the Punjab. Arguing that the government of India did not recognize Sikh concerns, the Akali Dal pushed for more independence for Punjab as a Sikh homeland. Each of these protest movements pointed to a growing feeling among Indian citizens that the government in Delhi overlooked and undervalued poor, minority, lower-caste, and lower-class Indians. Minority and undervalued Indian citizens began, and to this day continue, to question whether the Indian state sees them as part of the Indian nation.

## THIRD INDO-PAK WAR AND AN INDEPENDENT BANGLADESH

In addition to domestic unrest in the early 1970s, another war between India and Pakistan was brewing. This time the conflict focused on India's border with what was then East Pakistan (now Bangladesh). In the 1947 partition, Pakistan was created out of the Muslim-majority provinces of British India, which were located in the northwest of India and in the eastern half of Bengal, making Pakistan a country divided by India. Although both East and West Pakistan had Muslim-majority populations, they had little in common culturally, socially, or linguistically. After independence, most of the power and the seat of government was in the western part of Pakistan, despite the fact that more of the population lived in East Pakistan. The Pakistani government banned the teaching of Bengali language—the regional language of East Pakistan—refused to recognize Bengali holidays, and concentrated aid and economic development in West Pakistan. Journalists in East Pakistan argued that they were essentially being colonized by West Pakistan.[13]

The 1970 Pakistani elections brought the conflict between East and West Pakistan to the fore. For the first time, an East Pakistani political party won the general elections. Yahya Khan, the military dictator located in West Pakistan, refused to accept the election results. He began a military buildup in East Pakistan and helped to instigate a series of police actions targeting leaders, teachers, and minority Bengali Hindu populations in East Pakistan, accusing them of being rebels. Refugees poured into the Indian state of West Bengal across the border from East Pakistan. Indira Gandhi began a press tour to bring attention to the situation in East Pakistan, while Yahya Khan, the military leader in Pakistan argued that India had been training East Pakistani fighters to destabilize Pakistan. By the end of 1971, Gandhi pledged Indian military support to the East Pakistani fighters, and West Pakistan began a military action across the Kashmiri Line of Control—the de facto international border in Kashmir—hoping to capitalize on Indian commitments to fight in East Pakistan to take Kashmir. Indian airstrikes firmly defended the line of control with Pakistan in Kashmir, while the joint Indian and East Pakistani fighters successfully repelled the West Pakistan army in the east. In the end, East Pakistan was granted independence and became Bangladesh, and India solidified its status as the main military power in South Asia for several

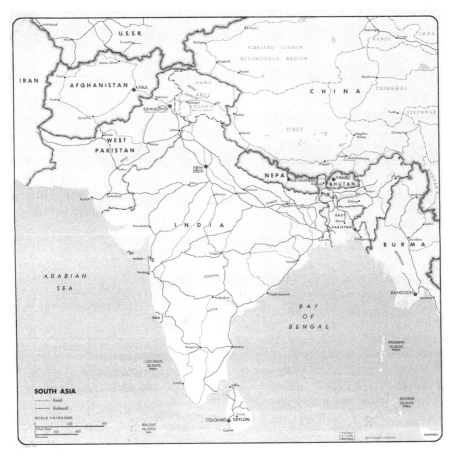

Map 7.1. Map of South Asia, 1960s, with Pakistan highlighted.
Source: Wikimedia Commons, https://commons.wikimedia.org/
wiki/File:1963_South_Asia_(30249403993).jpg.

decades. Bangladesh suffered more than two million civilian casualties, with at
least twice that many refugees resettled in India.[14]

## EMERGENCY AND ITS AFTERMATH

In the 1972 general election, the Congress Party won a decisive victory. The
opposing Janata Party challenged Indira Gandhi's district election, claiming that
she had engaged in voter fraud. In May 1975, the Indian Supreme Court ruled
that Gandhi had indeed acted improperly and nullified her election, essentially
removing her from the legislature. In June 1975, Gandhi asked the president of
India to declare a constitutional emergency, pointing to domestic national unrest

as the reason for the unprecedented action. Emergency powers, as defined by article 352 of the constitution, allowed for constitutional rights to be suspended for a limited time on the basis of external war or internal threats to the nation. It allowed the prime minister to suspend the legislative session, overrule the Supreme Court, and declare martial law.[15]

In June 1975, Indira Gandhi assumed emergency powers. The period of emergency powers lasted until March 1977. Almost immediately, Gandhi and the remaining government ministers began a crackdown on civil and political society. Political opposition leaders were arrested, including the leaders of the Janata Party, Total Revolution, and Akali Dal. Newspapers were shut down or had their content strictly censored. Other media outlets, particularly state radio and television stations, were reprogrammed to emphasize government positions. Gandhi deliberately retained a limited group of trusted advisors, including her sons and other family members.

Soon after declaring an emergency, Gandhi announced a series of poverty-reduction measures that seemed to rebrand policies from the Total Revolution Movement, the Anti-Price Rise movement, the Chipko movement, and others. Land reforms, price reductions on staples, ending bonded labor, and afforestation policies—planting trees in areas that had no previous forests—were all proposed. While welcome reforms, these new policies were inconsistently and often corruptly enforced. Moreover, the government often treated citizen complaints about the policies or their implementation as threats against the regime that could lead to prison or worse. Gandhi's emergency acts also included crackdowns on labor movements and strikes, a government policy of forced sterilization, and slum clearances, all of which were directed against the poor.[16]

By 1976, Gandhi had walled herself off from criticism, and advisors and friends told her that she was likely to win a general election if she lifted emergency regulations and reinstituted the parliament. The elections of 1977 did not go as Gandhi planned. Congress and Gandhi lost to a reconstituted Janata Party that collected all of Gandhi's political rivals from the right and the left. The coalition had little in common besides a desire to remove Gandhi from power. Moraji Desai became the first non-Congress Party prime minister, and the new government immediately changed the rules to make emergency almost impossible to do again. After changing the emergency provisions in the constitution, the Janata Party coalition began to crumble. By 1978, Desai was forced to resign after a successful vote of no confidence, and general elections were called for in 1979. In those elections, Indira Gandhi and the Congress Party once again won a solid majority, and Gandhi was reinstated as prime minister, with her son Sanjay Gandhi as head of the Congress Party.

Figure 7.2. The Golden Temple in Amritsar. Source: Photo by Ken Wieland, reproduced under a creative commons license, Wikimedia Commons, https://commons.wikimedia.org/wiki/File:Golden_Temple_ reflecting_in_the_Sarovar,_Amritsar.jpg.

## SIKH SEPARATISM AND INDIRA GANDHI'S ASSASSINATION

After the Emergency, the Sikh political party, the Akali Dal, released a series of demands, some of which were precursors to Sikh separatism and others that indicated an interest in Sikhs being understood as Indians. In 1980, some of the more extreme Akali Dal leaders declared the Punjab to be an independent Sikh nation and began a series of actions against the Indian government. By 1984, Sikh separatists began to stockpile weapons at the Golden Temple in Amritsar. The Golden Temple, the most holy temple in the Sikh religion, is a popular pilgrimage site for Sikhs from around the world. Thousands of people visit the temple daily. The leaders of the separatists used the crowds to mask their activities. Indian law permits religious sites to act as self-governing spaces if they do not bar entry because of caste or gender. Generally, police officers and army personal are only permitted to come into religious spaces for personal reasons (for example, worship) or if officials of the religious site ask them to enter.

In early June 1984, Gandhi's government began Operation Bluestar, a raid on the Golden Temple to capture stockpiled weapons and arrest Sikh separatist leaders. When the raid was over, the government claimed they had collected a large cache of weapons, but eighty-three soldiers, and 492 Sikhs inside the temple, had been killed. Eyewitness accounts suggest that the number of the dead was higher than reported and that some who were killed were innocent bystanders.[17] The temple complex was also damaged. The raids had the effect of alienating a significant portion of the Sikh population. Shortly after the raids, government officials suggested that Prime Minister Gandhi remove Sikhs from her personal bodyguard team, but she refused, indicating the action would heighten feelings of mistrust between the Sikh community and her government.

On October 31, 1984, two of Gandhi's Sikh bodyguards shot and killed her as she was leaving the prime minister's residence. Gandhi's assassination resulted in four days of nationwide riots against the Sikhs; they were especially fierce in New Delhi. Rioters, shouting slogans like "Blood for blood," killed more than 3,500 Sikhs, and police were encouraged to stand by and let the riots run their course.[18] Rajiv Gandhi, the son of Indira Gandhi, took over as prime minister. After four days of rioting, he finally deployed riot police to quell the violence. The effects of the riots, and the unwillingness of the government to protect the Sikhs, alienated many Indians. Sikh perceptions of second-class citizenship would continue with the 1990s rise of Hindu nationalism.

# 8

# India in a New Century, 1985–2010

The end of the Emergency, the expansion of political parties beyond Congress, and the waning Cold War globally made the 1980s to the 2010s a period of significant change in India. Economically, the Indian government transitioned from a highly controlled economy focused on self-sufficiency and limited foreign investment to a substantially less government-regulated economy with private and public sector decision-makers cultivating global markets and foreign investment. From 1991, when the government opened the economy, until the mid-2000s, economic growth surged, building a significant middle class and raising many out of poverty.[1] Although the realization of the new policies lifted millions of people out of poverty, there were unintended negative consequences for many other Indian citizens.

Increasingly, the unevenness of Indian economic growth after 1992 made poor Indians and agrarian communities feel left behind or forgotten in conversations about Indian prosperity. Politically, the rise of different political parties and ideologies—notably, regional parties and, perhaps most significantly, Hindu nationalist parties—made questions about what it meant to be Indian contentious. Moves to include more Dalits, women, and other minorities in Indian political and social lives were bringing new people and methods into Indian political activism. At the same time, the rise of Hindu nationalist political parties made many Indians feel not just excluded but endangered.

## Economic Development and Liberalization

Before the early 1980s, the Indian government had a structured, planned economy emphasizing self-sufficiency and minimizing imports. The government controlled imports, exports, and manufacturing, and it imposed high tariffs to encourage Indian manufacturing. Foreign investment in India was strictly limited, and the

Indian rupee was held on a fixed exchange rate. By the late 1970s, India began to have financial problems, both within the country and with trading partners. Some Indians began to call for the government to open the economy to more foreign investment and allow for less regulation of production in the face of the scarcity of goods and services. Additionally, aid organizations, like the World Bank and the International Monetary Fund (IMF), urged India to restructure its often-stagnant government-planned economy. The 1980s saw the beginning of a shift in the Indian economy, but widespread economic liberalization was mostly accomplished after 1991. In 1991, in order to avoid complete economic collapse, the Indian Ministry of Finance enacted a series of policies meant to open the Indian economy. The economic restructuring was led by Manmohan Singh, who was then finance minister.

Singh, educated in England and internationally focused, saw economic deregulation as the means to bring India more significantly into the global economy. A Sikh at a time when Sikhs were still actively mistrusted, Singh eventually became the prime minister of India from 2004 to 2014. As part of the country's economic liberalization in 1991, the government floated the rupee and allowed for higher levels of direct foreign investment. It also largely dismantled government monopolies in industries to allow for more competition. India's economic transition resulted in an estimated 271 million people escaping poverty. It is also notable that in sharp contrast to China's leaders, who also garnered the attention of the world for market-oriented policies that significantly reduced poverty, India's transition was accomplished with a clear mandate to safeguard its democratic institutions. The policies of economic liberalization have contributed to India's current reputation as one of the most stable and upcoming economies in the world.

Still, the shift in economic systems had uneven effects. Generally, GDP has risen consistently, as has foreign direct investment in Indian corporations and industry.[2] The percentage of people living below the poverty line has decreased significantly since 1980.[3] Urban middle-class areas have clearly benefited from cheaper and more plentiful imports, less expensive construction material, and, in some cases, more jobs. The effect on agriculture, urban poverty, and rural areas has been much less positive. With the government providing fewer subsidies for agricultural inputs like seeds and fertilizers, farmers were not able to sustain their farms through bad growing seasons. A rash of farmer suicides in the late 1990s and early 2000s brought some attention to the problems of agrarian indebtedness and their relationship to the policies of economic liberalization.[4] In addition, wealth and income inequality have both risen significantly since economic liberalization.[5] Farmers, poor Indians, and people living in poverty-ridden areas have often felt left out of, or even the victims of, Indian prosperity.[6]

Women have also been, for the most part, left out of the economic changes in India. Fewer than 40 percent of working-age women in India were working in the formal economy in 2023. Women's participation in the formal workforce has been hampered by family pressures and shortages of jobs across the board. Often, men are given preference over women applicants.[7] But the issue is also complicated by the persistence of the large informal economic sector. Domestic labor and childcare—both of which are primarily done by women and are often paid outside formal labor arrangements—generally go unreported and unregulated.

Many Indians would also like to see stronger labor and environment laws and better and more uniform enforcement of those laws to protect vulnerable populations and ecosystems. The 1984 Union Carbide gas leak in Bhopal, which occurred before India's change in economic direction, killed more than eight thousand people over two weeks; it continues to contaminate groundwater in that area. Although the Indian Supreme Court found Union Carbide and their officials liable for the loss of life and the ongoing health crisis in Bhopal, survivors have never been properly compensated. Other, less deadly industrial accidents have pointed to the need to balance economic development with the values of safe work environments and environmental stewardship.[8] Activists have urged the government to work with local communities when opening space for economic development, building dams, or creating new industries to ensure that a wider swath of Indians benefit from economic growth, or at least that Indians from minority and marginalized communities are not actively harmed by economic development. Nongovernmental organizations (NGOs) and activist groups have also worked with farmers and the poor to try to address the lack of government support, especially in the period since economic liberalization. While NGOs and activist networks have sometimes been able to secure land rights, build functional schools, and help protect traditional rights to forest materials, they are not a complete substitute for government aid and attention.[9]

## POLITICAL AND SOCIAL CHANGE AT THE TURN OF THE TWENTY-FIRST CENTURY

If the turn of the twentieth century in India was marked by the founding of anti-colonial political parties that would come to lead the movement for Indian independence, the turn to the twenty-first century marked the reinvigoration of Hindu nationalism in Indian political life. For many Indians, Hinduism is a religion with an important and firmly held belief system. Significant numbers of Hindus employ religious institutions, traditions, belief systems, and communities in an attempt to make the world a better place; examples range from charitable actions, such as feeding the poor, to offering support for Hindu communities. Hinduism, like most other religions, offers a support, guidance, comfort, and community for its believers, and encourages peaceful and positive change in the world.

Hindu nationalism, in contrast, is a political ideology whose adherents insist India should be a homeland primarily for Hindus, with many nationalists indicating that only Hindus are genuine Indians. For ardent Hindu nationalist adherents and politicians, people of other religions—primarily Muslims but also Christians and, in some regions, Sikhs—are visitors, and sometimes unwelcome visitors, in India. Hindu nationalism has been part of India's political discourse since well before independence. Before the late 1980s, however, overtly Hindu nationalist parties had not been very successful in national politics.

Because the assassination of Mohandas "Mahatma" Gandhi was carried out in the name of Hindu nationalism, for a short period after independence, Hindu nationalist organizing groups—like the Rashtriya Swayamsevak Sangh (RSS), roughly translated as "National Volunteer Organization," and the Hindu Mahasabha, or Hindu Assembly—were banned. Even after they were reinstated, these parties were out of the mainstream. This relegation of Hindu nationalist parties does not mean Hindu nationalist ideas were only embraced by a small number of people. Many members of Congress professed Hindu nationalist ideas, and the Hindu religion has often been conflated with political-majority parties in India. Instead, it can be argued that until the early 1980s, the establishment, including political leaders, the media, and academics, frowned upon overt Hindu nationalist organizing.

By the middle of the 1980s, several things had changed that allowed Hindu nationalism, overt anti-Muslim sentiments, and, often, violence to seem like viable, winning political strategies. Hindu nationalists used the populist movements of the 1970s to reframe the idea of Indian democracy as fundamentally linked to the Hindu majority. By claiming that Indian Muslims were outsiders, traitors, and leeches on the national wealth, Hindu nationalists used the upheaval caused by the economic downturn of the 1980s and early 1990s to popularize the idea of India as a Hindu country.[10] Leaders of Hindu nationalist political parties have argued that Congress especially—but left-wing political parties in general—has pandered to minorities to make the place of Hindu people in the country less secure. The founding of the Bharatiya Janata Party (BJP) as an explicitly and primarily Hindu nationalist party created a political outlet that could win elections with the backing of civil and political organizations—the RSS and its Sangh Parivar, or "family of organizations."

One issue that brought Hindu nationalist organizing to the fore and made the BJP into a successful national party was organizing for a Ram temple in Ayodhya. Beginning in 1985, the RSS and other Hindu nationalist parties began a movement to build a Ram temple on the site of the Babri Masjid, an early sixteenth-century mosque that Hindu nationalist organizers argued was built on the birthplace of the Hindu god Ram. Although previous disputes occurred about the mosque and the land surrounding it, including the rights of both Muslims and Hindus to worship at the site, the issue became a rallying cry for Hindu nationalist politics in the early 1990s.[11]

The RSS and the Vishva Hindu Parishad (VHP)—another Hindu nationalist organization—created pilgrimages to bring bricks to Ayodhya to build a new Ram temple on the site of the existing mosque. Pilgrims often carried signs and shouted slogans that violently expressed the idea that India was a Hindu country and that

Figure 8.1. Babri Masjid, before it was demolished by rioters in 1992. Source: Wikimedia Commons, https://commons.wikimedia.org/wiki/Category:Babri_ Masjid#/media/File:Babri_Masjid.jpg.

others were unwelcome. "There is only one place for Muslims, Pakistan or the graveyard" constitutes a particularly egregious example.[12] The pilgrimages were often the source of violence and rioting between Hindu and Muslim communities. By 1992, the rhetoric grew to a fever pitch. On December 6, 1992, a meeting was held at the site of the mosque. Leaders from the RSS, BJP, and VHP claimed India as a Hindu nation and cited the Babri Masjid as a physical representation of the "invasion" of Muslims into India. The crowd stormed past the fencing protecting the mosque and demolished it.[13] Riots between Hindus and Muslims broke out all over the country but primarily in the state of Uttar Pradesh, where the mosque was located, and in Bombay (now Mumbai) where over nine hundred people were killed. The BJP was able to turn the years of virulent anti-Muslim rhetoric and communal violence into electoral success, winning ever-larger vote counts and, ultimately in 1998, majorities in the federal parliamentary elections, making Atal Bihari Vajpayee the prime minister. In 1999, a border skirmish between Indians and Pakistanis, the Kargil conflict, reignited the Hindu nationalist rhetoric of Muslims as outsiders in India and turned Hindu nationalist rhetoric into an overt strategy on the Indian political right.

The success of Hindu nationalism as an electoral strategy, especially after significant violence, was troubling for many Indians, both Hindus and non-Hindus, who found the conflation of India with Hinduism unsettling. It was especially so because the BJP continued to promote actions that made non-Hindus and Hindus who believed in secularism and diversity uncomfortable. The government began to modify the history textbooks for grade school students to highlight Hinduism as the religion and culture of India.[14]

The government also turned a blind eye to increasing intimidation and violence against religious minorities. This came to a head in 2002 in Gujarat, a state along India's west coast. On February 27, 2002, two train cars carrying Hindus returning from a pilgrimage to Ayodhya were set on fire at Godhra. Fifty-seven people, mostly Hindus, were killed. How the train fire started is a matter of public uncertainty. Two official commissions found significantly different answers. The Nanavati-Mehta Commission claimed that a Muslim group intentionally set fire to the train, while another group, the Banerjee Commission, argued that the fire was an accident.[15] In either case, Hindu nationalist organizers encouraged their supporters to retaliate to what they saw as communal violence and helped to organize a violent response.[16] More than nine hundred Muslims were killed, and at least 150,000 were displaced by the rioting.[17] Gujarat Chief Minister Modi used these riots as an election opportunity, campaigning on the importance of celebrating India as a Hindu nation. He won reelection in December of 2002 and would later rise in the BJP to become the prime minister of India in 2014. The rise of Hindu nationalism has become an effective and popular political strategy that has resonated with many people, but it has also made many other people feel unwelcome and unsafe in their own country. Muslims, Christians, Dalits, and other minorities have all seen the government turn a blind eye to Hindu nationalist violence against their communities.

## RETHINKING CASTE, CLASS, AND GENDER POLITICS

Although the rise of Hindu nationalism is the main political narrative of the 1980s through the 2010s, other major political movements are also key to understanding this period in Indian history. One of the most interesting is the rise of the Bahujan Samaj Party (BSP), a party focused on raising the political profile of lower-caste peoples. The BSP was started in 1984 by Kanshi Ram, a Dalit social and political activist. Ram's objective was to mobilize the Dalit population, the Adivasis (Indian indigenous people), and other low-caste people, who make up more than 70 percent of India's population when they band together. Engaged by the political thought of Ambedkar, Phule, and others, Ram's party was quickly successful in Northern India, and especially in Uttar Pradesh. By 1990, the BSP was an important part of political life in Uttar Pradesh, with Ram elected to the government in 1994. Ram's political successor, Mayawati, was elected chief minister of Uttar Pradesh in 1995. Mayawati was the first Dalit woman to be elected to the post of chief minister in India.[18] Another important political shift of the 1980s through the turn of the twenty-first century is the continued dominance of regionally organized political parties, particularly in Southern India. Political parties focused on specific

Figure 8.2. Statues of Mayawati and Kanshi Ram at Ambedkar Park in Lucknow. Source: Wikimedia Commons, https://commons.wikimedia.org/wiki/File:Image_of_India.jpg.

regional concerns have continued to be part of major party coalitions in federal election cycles.

The rise of political populism in the late 1970s also fueled new women's political efforts. The 1980s and 1990s offered some wins for Indian women, both in the legislative arena and in their activism outside of electoral politics. In 1993, the government passed a constitutional amendment requiring that women hold at least one-third of leadership positions in village governments around India. Bills to extend those quotas to state and national government were brought forward but have remained stalled. Women's rights activists also worked to make changes in the laws governing the prosecution of rape. They sought to change rules that allowed the defense to undermine a woman's charge of rape if it could be proven that the woman could be classified as a person of immoral character. In 2003, the rules allowing for immorality defenses were repealed, although they are still in de facto use today.[19] Despite these important legislative wins for women, many women's rights activists felt that a focus on changing culture was at least as important as changing laws. They began to push back against attempts to police their ability to move around in public, dress as they felt fit, speak, and participate in society. Similarly, movements by LGBTQIA Indians began during the late 1990s and early 2000s. They pushed for the government to repeal section 377 of the Indian penal code, which criminalized homosexual activity, while also arguing for the rights of Indian LGBTQIA citizens to live openly and in public.[20]

The Indian northeast has a troubled relationship with the Indian federal government that began even before independence, and the 1980s, 1990s, and

Figure 8.3. Protesting section 377, which criminalized homosexuality in India, in 2018. Source: Sailesh Patnaik, Wikimedia Commons, https://commons.wikimedia.org/wiki/ File:Bhubaneswar_Pride_Parade_2018_02.jpg.

early 2000s included a slight rise in regional separatist activity. Because the central government designated much of the northeast as uncivil and dangerous to national security, the military police, violence, and a lack of resources sparked calls for better treatment in the northeast or else it would lead to separation from India. By 1990, most of the Indian northeast has been under the Armed Forces Special Powers Act, which gives the Indian army special powers to search, detain, and even bodily harm or kill anyone they see as a threat to the Indian nation without threat of discipline.[21] Recent shifts in policies around policing and better relations between the northeastern states and the central government led to both reduced insurgency activity and fewer military outrages, but many Indians still consider citizens from northeastern states less wholly Indian than citizens from other areas.

Between the 1980s and the 2010s, Indian leaders changed the way the economy, politics, and society were oriented. Economic liberalization built a new middle class and sparked economic development, although the effects were uneven. New political organizing meant that Muslims, Dalits, women, and the poor all saw their space in society negated significantly, despite having nowhere else to belong.

# Conclusion

## Being Indian in the Twenty-First Century

For a variety of factors, including Prime Minister Modi's often authoritarian central government, the second decade of the twenty-first century has seen continually escalating attacks on Indian Muslims, Christians, Dalits, women, journalists, lawyers, students, farmers, and activists across India.[1] Similarly, the ongoing but undeclared martial law in Kashmir and Northeast India, the continued crackdown on Adivasis and Dalits in Chhattisgarh in the name of preventing Naxalite violence, and the stifling of the media has made dissent against the government very difficult.[2] The growth of pollution, quality of life concerns, and Indian megacities have continued to raise challenges for Indian citizens and the government. Yet many Indian citizens continue to push back and try to make meaningful changes in their country through voting, legal changes, media representation, and protest, even when these actions carry the threat of retaliation and personal danger.

Several civil rights campaigns were successful in bringing Supreme Court cases to change Indian laws early in the twenty-first century. In 2013, the Supreme Court affirmed the recognition of fundamental rights to a third gender category in India, allowing for hijras—an indigenous non-binary and transgender community—and other transgender people to access governmental resources like passports and revised birth certificates. In another landmark ruling in 2018, the Indian Supreme Court issued a verdict declaring it unconstitutional to criminalize homosexuality, after more than thirty years of fighting to end laws against sodomy and homosexuality.[3]

In the 2010s, the Indian legislature also passed several laws against sexual harassment in public, in the workplace, and in institutions of higher education. In 2013, a revision of the Indian rape laws was passed as a result of a series of harrowing and very public rape cases, after several decades of women's rights organizations advocated for the change.[4] Even these wins, however, have been less complete than many desire. Women, especially women from marginalized communities, still face significant difficulties filing a police report when they are the victims of sexual violence. Women, LGBTQIA people, and religious minorities like Muslims,

Sikhs, and Christians continue to battle harassment and discrimination in the street and workplace, and from police and other representatives of government. Discrimination and violence targeting Dalits based on their caste also remains prevalent.

As India's population continues to grow, issues related to crowding in megacities like New Delhi, Mumbai, and Kolkata—including air pollution, transportation availability, and access to medical care, food, and affordable energy—have become pressing. Increasingly, air pollution has caused health issues like increased rates of heart attacks and respiratory ailments, especially during the winter months. These issues affect everyone in India but are more pressing for poor people living in urban areas, who are forced to spend more time outdoors and who often do not have access to air purifiers and clean energy sources.[5] As India attempts to find a balance between development, urbanization, and quality of life, poor people often end up paying the price.

By the early twenty-first century, scholars were pointing to the BRICS—which stands for Brazil, Russia, India, China, and South Africa—as strongly developing economies that would likely influence global political and economic policy in the years to come. Each one of the BRICS nations is the dominant national power in their region, and they have broad economic and political ambitions abroad.[6] Although both India and China are members of the increasingly formal BRICS organization, the relationships between the two countries is unsettled. As has already been noted, India and China never resolved disputes about their shared border, with skirmishes happening periodically. China's strong relationship with Pakistan, and its increasing engagement with other countries in South Asia, has led India to feel less comfortable in its relationship with China.[7] At the same time, the relationship between the United States and India has become more robust, with India acting as an economic and political partner in the United States' interests in South Asia. As South Asia becomes more central to geopolitical and global economic concerns, India is becoming more central to international policy around the globe.

One of the major concerns since 2010 has been the ongoing attempt to crack down on dissent in India and the danger this poses to Indian democratic traditions and government. In 2016, the government began arresting activists as anti-nationals, focusing particularly on Dalits, Muslims, and their advocates who criticize the government. Several university professors and students were arrested in 2018, and well-known lawyers were arrested as anti-national agents through the Unlawful Activities (Prevention) Act, anti-terrorism legislation that short-circuits the normal rule of law. These changes—along with legislative moves, such as the Citizenship (Amendment) Act of 2019, that make India less welcoming to Muslims; civil society changes, like the opening of a Ram temple in Ayodhya at the site of the Babri Masjid; and ongoing government-supported violence against Muslims—have made many Indians feel uneasy about India's democracy and future. Upticks in violence against religious minorities, including Muslims (about 14 percent of the population, or over two hundred million people), Christians (about 4 percent of the population, or approximately seven million people), and Sikhs (about 2 percent of the population, or about 3.5 million people) have been associated with rising Hindu nationalist sentiment.[8] Christian services and religious leaders have been wrongly targeted by a number of states who have implemented anti-conversion laws as a way to stifle Christian religious practice in India. Like Islam, Christianity has a long history in India, with the first Christians arriving by the fourth century CE at the latest.[9] Periodic acts of violence occur against Christians, 74 percent of whom identify as Dalits.[10] Similarly, Muslim congregations and leaders have increasingly been the targets of state and state-supported violence, although they have been the target of state and societal violence since the nineteenth century.

From before independence until now, India has evinced a strong commitment to democratic processes. Freedom of expression, cultures of debate, and a willingness to allow for dissent and difference have been part of the vision of the nation that many Indians have professed. In places and times when these values have been undermined—during the Emergency, in Kashmir and the northeast, and in the growth of Hindu nationalist rhetoric at the turn of the twenty-first century—India's democratic governance and shared nationality have been shaken. While elections in India continue to nominally hit the threshold of "free and fair," the Modi government has been undermining institutions of democracy through its practices of jailing members of the press, removing opposition leaders from parliament, and menacing people who vocally dissent against government actions. These threats to democratic institutions have caused many organizations and scholars to cite India as an example of democratic backsliding and majoritarian rule. Freedom House, which publishes an annual index of freedom and democracy around the world, recategorized India in 2022 as only "partly free."[11]

Despite personal and professional danger involved in criticizing the government, farmers, students, journalists, activists, and scholars continue to protest the government's repression of democratic institutions. In the 2024 elections, tireless action on the part of activists and some sections of the media to discover government and BJP party corruption led to a much more tightly contested election than expected and a diminished majority for Modi and his coalition. The continued call for the renormalization of dissent, a free press, and peaceful if heated debate is the best sign that can be seen for the continuation and strengthening of India's democratic heritage.

In the next several decades, it will be necessary for India's people and government to confront issues of environmental change, political violence, and regional and global conflict as India and the world change. Understanding the history of the Indian nation can help readers to engage with current events as they arise. This volume is just the very tip of the iceberg for any of the topics discussed. Unlike the popular image of India as traditional and unchanging, India is dynamic and impossible to contain in a single narrative.

# NOTES

## INTRODUCTION

[1] Jhimli Mukherjee Pandey, "Indus Era 8,000 Years Old, Not 5,500; Ended Because of Weaker Monsoon," *Times of India*, May 29, 2016, https://timesofindia.indiatimes.com/india/indus-era-8000-years-old-not-5500-ended-because-of-weaker-monsoon/articleshow/52485332.cms.

## CHAPTER 1

[1] John F. Richards, *The Mughal Empire* (Cambridge: Cambridge University Press, 1993).

[2] Rosalind O'Hanlon, "Kingdom, Household, and Body History, Gender and Imperial Service under Akbar," *Modern Asian Studies* 41, no. 5 (2007): 889–923.

[3] Rekha Bandyopadhyay, "Land System in India: A Historical Review," *Economic and Political Weekly* 28, no. 52 (1993): A149–155.

[4] Nita Verma Prasad, "Manjhan's Madhumalati and the Construction of Indo-Islam," *Education about Asia* 25, no. 1 (Spring 2020): 48–54.

[5] Richards, *The Mughal Empire,* chapter 12.

[6] Ebba Koch, *Mughal Architecture* (New York: Prestal, 1991).

[7] Ali Anooshahr, "Science at the Court of the Cosmocrat: Mughal India, 1531–56," *Indian Economic and Social History Review* 54, no. 3: 295–316.

[8] Muzaffar Alam and Sanjay Subrahmanyam, *Writing the Mughal World: Studies on Culture and Politics* (New York: Columbia University Press, 2012).

## CHAPTER 2

[1] Atul Sethi, "Trade, Not Invasion Brought Islam to India," *Times of India*, June 24, 2007.

[2] V. K. Jain, "The Role of the Arab Traders in Western India during the Early Medieval Period," *Proceedings of the Indian History Congress* 39 (1978): 285–295.

[3] K. N. Chaudhuri, *Trade and Civilization in the Indian Ocean: An Economic History from the Rise of Islam to 1750* (Cambridge: Cambridge University Press, 1985).

[4] James M. Vaughn, "John Company Armed: The English East India Company, the Anglo-Mughal War and Absolutist Imperialism, c. 1675–1690," *Britain and the World* 11, no. 1 (2017): 101–137.

[5] Erin Blakemore, "How the East India Company Became the World's Most Powerful Business," *National Geographic*, September 6, 2019, https://www.nationalgeographic.com/culture/topics/reference/british-east-india-trading-company-most-powerful-business.

[6] For a quick note on the Battle of Plassey, see this blogpost from the British National Army Museum: "Battle of Plassey," National Army Museum, https://www.nam.ac.uk/explore/battle-plassey.

[7] Nicholas Dirks, *The Scandal of Empire: India and the Creation of Imperial Britain* (Cambridge: Harvard University Press, 2006).

[8] John F. Richards, *The Mughal Empire* (Cambridge: Cambridge University Press, 1993).

[9] Philip Lawson, *The East India Company: A History* (Harlow: Longman, 1993).

[10] Barbara Metcalf and Thomas Metcalf, *A Concise History of Modern India*, 2nd ed. (Cambridge: Cambridge University Press, 2006).

[11] Michael Fisher, "Indirect Rule in the British Empire: The Foundations of the Residency System in India," *Modern Asian Studies* 18, no. 3 (1984): 393–428.

[12] Biswamoy Pati, ed., *The 1857 Rebellion* (New Delhi: Oxford University Press, 2007).

[13] Biswamoy Pati, ed. *The 1857 Rebellion*.

[14] R. C. Majumdar, *The Sepoy Mutiny and the Revolt of 1857* (Calcutta: Firma K. L. Mukhopadhyay, 1963).

## CHAPTER 3

[1] Nazmul S. Sultan, "Self-Rule and the Problem of Peoplehood in Colonial India," *American Political Science Review* 114, no. 1 (2020): 18–94.

[2] Rohan Deb Roy, "Decolonise Science: The Untold Story of Modern Science Is One of Empire and Colonial Exploitation," *Quartz India*, April 9, 2018, https://qz.com/india/1247577/the-untold-story-of-modern-science-is-one-of-empire-and-colonial-exploitation/.

[3] Dipesh Chakrabarty, "Postcoloniality and the Artifice of History: Who Speaks for 'Indian' Pasts?" *Representations* 37 (Winter 1992): 1–26.

[4] Thomas Macaulay, "Minute on Indian Education (February 2, 1835)," in *Speeches by Lord Macaulay with His Minute on Indian Education*, edited by G. M. Young (London: Oxford University Press, 1935), 345–361.

[5] Partha Chatterjee, "Colonialism, Nationalism, and the Colonized Woman in India," *American Ethnologist* 16, no. 4 (1989): 622–633.

[6] Barbara D. and Thomas Metcalf, *A Concise History of Modern India*, 3rd ed. (Cambridge: Cambridge University Press, 2012).

[7] Rosalind O'Hanlon, *Caste, Conflict, and Ideology: Mahatma Jotirao Phule and Low-Caste Protest in Nineteenth-Century Western India* (Cambridge: Cambridge University Press, 1985).

[8] Gopalkrishna Gandhi, "A Newspaper with a View," *Hindustan Times*, October 1, 2020, https://www.hindustantimes.com/india-news/a-newspaper-with-a-view/story-3ahbm3g8GbCY07P3f2OCuN.html.

[9] Pamela Hutchinson, "The Birth of India's Film Industry: How the Movies Came to Mumbai," *Guardian*, July 25, 2013, https://www.theguardian.com/film/2013/jul/25/birth-indias-film-industry-movies-mumbai.

[10] Jayati Bhattacharya, "The Story of Indian Business: The Great Transition into the New Millennium," *Education about Asia* 24, no. 2 (Fall 2019): 22–27; Utsa Patnaik, "India in the World Economy, 1900–1930: The Inter-War Depression and Britain's Demise as a World Capitalist Leader," *Social Scientist* 42, no. 1/2 (Jan–Feb 2014): 13–35.

[11] Sekhar Bandyopadhyay, *From Plassey to Partition: A History of Modern India* (Hyderabad: Orient Blackswan, 2005); Shabnum Tejani, *Indian Secuarlism: A Social and Intellectual History, 1890–1950* (Bloomington: Indiana University Press, 2008).

[12] M. Rafique Afzal, *A History of the All-India Muslim League, 1906–1947* (Karachi: Oxford University Press, 2014).

[13] Metcalf and Metcalf, *Concise History of Modern India*, 3rd ed., 155.

[14] Amrita Gupta Singh, "1905: Cartography, Nationalism, and Iconography," *Partition Studies Quarterly* 2 (2020), http://www.partitionstudiesquarterly.org/article/1905-cartography-nationalism-and-iconography/.

[15] Bal Gangadhar Tilak, "Address to the Indian National Congress, 1907," reprinted in William T. de Bary, *Sources of Indian Tradition* (New York: Columbia University Press, 1958), 719–723.

# CHAPTER 4

[1] Vedica Kant, *"If I Die Here, Who Will Remember Me?" India and the First World War* (New Delhi: Roli Books, 2015); "Why the Indian Soldiers of World War I Were Forgotten," BBC.com, July 2, 2015, https://www.bbc.com/news/magazine-33317368.

[2] Amiya Kumar Bagchi, "Indian Economy and Society during World War One," *Social Scientist* 43, no. 7/8 (2014): 5–27.

[3] Emily Rook-Koepsel, "Dissenting against the Defence of India Rules: Extralegal Regulations and the Space of Extreme Government Action," *South Asia: Journal of South Asian Studies* 41, no. 3 (2018): 642–657.

[4] The whole text of Gandhi's *Hind Swaraj*, or *Indian Home Rule*, originally published in 1909, can be found at mkgandhi.org: https://www.mkgandhi.org/ebks/hind_swaraj.pdf.

[5] Gandhi wrote extensively on satyagraha, especially in his newspapers, *Young India* and the *Harijan*. Here is an excerpt of some of these writings in the *Selected Writing of Mahatma Gandhi*: "The Practice of Satyagraha or Civil Disobedience," Comprehensive Website on the Life and Works of Mahatma Gandhi, https://www.mkgandhi.org/swmgandhi/chap03.htm.

[6] T. C. A. Raghavan, "1919: A Portrait," *Open Magazine*, December 20, 2018, https://openthemagazine.com/cover-stories/new-year-2019-issue/1919-a-portrait/.

[7] Shahid Amin, *Event, Metaphor, Memory: Chauri Chaura 1922–1992* (Berkeley: University of Press, 1995).

[8] M. Naeem Qureshi, *Pan-Islam in British Indian Politics: A Study of the Khilafat Movement, 1918–1924* (Leiden: Brill, 1999).

[9] Bala Jeyaraman, *Periyar: A Political Biography of E. V. Ramasamy* (New Delhi: Rupa Publications, 2013).

[10] B. R. Ambedkar, *What Congress and Gandhi Have Done to the Untouchables* (Bombay: Thacker, 1945).

[11] Sumit Sarkar and Tanika Sarkar, eds. *Women and Social Reform in Modern India: A Reader* (Bloomington: Indiana University Press, 2008).

[12] Radha Kumar, *History of Doing: An Illustrated Account of Movements for Women's Rights and Feminism in India, 1800–1990* (New Delhi: Kali for Women, 2002).

[13] Jawaharlal Nehru, "Birthday Letter," from *Glimpses of World History: Being Further Letters to His Daughter, Written in Prison, and Containing a Rambling*

*Account of History for Young People.* Full text on the Internet Archive: https://archive.org/stream/in.ernet.dli.2015.202084/2015.202084.Glimpses-Of_djvu.txt.

[14] The purna swaraj resolution may be read at the following link: "Declaration of Purna Swaraj (India National Congress, 1930)," Constitution of India, https://www.constitutionofindia.net/historical_constitutions/declaration_of_purna_swaraj__indian_national_congress__1930__26th%20January%201930.

[15] Gopalkrishna Gandhi, "The Great Dandi March—Eighty Years After," *The Hindu*, April 5, 2010, https://www.thehindu.com/opinion/op-ed/The-Great-Dandi-March-mdash-eighty-years-after/article16364352.ece.

[16] Barbara D. Metcalf and Thomas Metcalf, *A Concise History of Modern India*, 3rd ed. (Cambridge: Cambridge University Press, 2012).

[17] Muhammad Iqbal's 1930 presidential address can be found here: "Presidential Address by Muhamad Ali Jinnah to the Muslim League, Lahore, 1940, franpritchett.com, https://franpritchett.com/00islamlinks/txt_jinnah_lahore_1940.html.

[18] Ayesha Jalal, *The Sole Spokesman: Jinnah, the Muslim League, and the Demand for Pakistan*, (Cambridge: Cambridge University Press, 1985).

## CHAPTER 5

[1] Maria Abi-Habib, "The Forgottten Colonial Forces of World War II," *New York Times Magazine*, September 1, 2020, https://www.nytimes.com/2020/09/01/magazine/the-forgotten-colonial-forces-of-world-war-ii.html.

[2] Yasmin Khan, *The Raj at War: A People's History of India's Second World War* (London: Bodley Head, 2015); Srinath Raghavan, *India's War: The Making of Modern South Asia, 1939–1945* (London: Allen Lane, 2016).

[3] Emily Rook-Koepsel, "Dissenting against the Defence of India Rules: Extralegal Regulations and the Space of Extreme Government Action," *South Asia: Journal of South Asian Studies* 41, no 3 (2018): 642–657.

[4] Chandar S. Sundaram, "Trial at the Red Fort 1945–1946: The Indian National Army and the End of the British Raj in India," *EAA* 27, no. 3 (Winter 2022): 12–20.

[5] Amaryta Sen, "Famines," *World Development* 8, no. 9 (September 1980): 613–621.

[6] Muhammad Ali Jinnah's presidential address to the 1940 All-India Muslim League Conference can be read here: "Presidential address by Muhammad Ali Jinnah to the Muslim League, Lahore, 1940," franpritchett.com, https://franpritchett.com/00islamlinks/txt_jinnah_lahore_1940.html.

[7] Ikran Ali Malik, *Muslim League Session 1940 and the Lahore Resolution: Documents* (Islamabad: National Institute of Historical and Culture Research, 1990).

[8] Karthik Venkatesh, "All but Forgotten: Choudhary Rahmat Ali, the Inventor and First Champion of Pakistan," *Wire*, February 20, 2018, https://thewire.in/history/choudhary-rahmat-ali-the-inventor-of-pakistan.

[9] Gandhi's "Quit India" speech can be read here: "The 'Quit India' Speech (8.8.1942)," Comprehensive Website on the Life and Works of Mahatma Gandhi, https://www.mkgandhi.org/speeches/qui.htm.

[10] Emily Rook-Koepsel, *Democracy and Unity in India: 1940–1960* (London: Routledge, 2019).

[11] Renuka Ray, "Wanted—Social Workers," *Roshni* 2, no. 4 (December 1940): 29–34.

[12] Muhammad Ali Jinnah, *The Dawn*, December 15, 1946, 7.

[13] Claude Markovits, "The Calcutta Riots of 1946," In *Online Encyclopedia of Mass Violence and Resistance*, Sciences Po, November 5, 2007, https://www.sciencespo.fr/mass-violence-war-massacre-resistance/en/document/calcutta-riots-1946.html.

[14] Anhad Hundal, "Getting the Picture: The Mystery of an Iconic Partition Photograph," *Caravan*, August 31, 2016, https://caravanmagazine.in/lede/getting-the-picture-iconic-partition-photograph.

[15] "Partition at 70: The Numbers that Divided India and Pakistan," *Hindustan Times*, August 14, 2017, https://www.hindustantimes.com/india-news/partition-at-70-the-numbers-that-divided-india-and-pakistan/story-KvuFkeJlqNBky3JT5ZaZuK.html.

[16] Gyanendra Pandey, "Community and Violence: Recalling Partition," *Economic and Political Weekly* 32, no. 32 (August 9, 1997): 2037–2039, 2041, 2045.

[17] Jawaharlal Nehru's "Tryst with Destiny" speech can be read or listened to here: Jawaharlal Nehru, "A Tryst with Destiny," *Guardian*, April 30, 2007, https://www.theguardian.com/theguardian/2007/may/01/greatspeeches. Muhammad Ali Jinnah's presidential address to the Constituent Assembly of Pakistan can be found here: "Muhammad Ali Jinnah's First Presidential Address to the Constituent Assembly of Pakistan (August 11, 1947)," franpritchett.com, https://franpritchett.com/00islamlinks/txt_jinnah_assembly_1947.html.

[18] Anjali Bhardwaj Datta, "Nation and Its 'Other' Women: Muslim Subjectivity and Gendered Agency in Delhi," *South Asia: Journal of South Asian Studies* 44, no. 2 (2021): 380–397.

[19] Balraj Puri, "Indian Muslims since Partition," *Economic and Political Weekly* 28, no. 40 (October 2, 1993): 2141–2149.

[20] UK Department for Business and Trade, "India Trade and Investment Factsheet," https://assets.publishing.service.gov.uk/media/6580590f83ba38000de1b7ba/india-trade-and-investment-factsheet-2023-12-21.pdf.

## CHAPTER 6

[1] Madhav Khosa, *India's Founding Moment: The Constitution of a Most Surprising Democracy* (Cambridge: Harvard University Press, 2020); Granville Austin, *The Indian Constitution: Cornerstone of a Nation* (Oxford: Oxford University Press, 1999).

[2] Ornit Shani, *How India Became Democratic: Citizenship and the Making of the Universal Franchise* (Cambridge: Cambridge University Press, 2017).

[3] "Rare Images of Independent India's First General Election," *Scroll.in*, April, 7, 2014, https://scroll.in/article/659860/rare-images-of-independent-indias-first-general-election-in-1952; Tripti Lahiri, "A Short History of the Congress Hand," *Wall Street Journal*, March 28, 2012, https://www.wsj.com/articles/BL-IRTB-14970.

[4] The Indian government dissolved their planning commission after their twelfth plan, which ran through 2017. Santosh Mehrotra and Sylvia Guichard, *Planning in the Twentieth Century and Beyond: India's Planning Commission and the NITI Aayog* (Cambridge: Cambridge University Press, 2020).

[5] Barbara Metcalf and Thomas Metcalf, *A Concise History of Modern India*, 2nd ed. (Cambridge: Cambridge University Press, 2006).

[6] Tripurdaman Singh, *Sixteen Stormy Days: The Story of the First Amendment to the Constitution of India* (New Delhi: Vintage, Penguin Random House, 2020).

[7] Jessica Chandras, "Multilingualism in India," *Education about Asia* 25, no. 3 (Winter 2020): 38–45.

[8] Taylor C. Sherman, "The Integration of the Princely State of Hyderabad and the Making of the Postcolonial State in India, 1948–1956," *Indian Economic and Social History Review* 44, no. 4 (December 2007): 489–516.

[9] Sumantra Bose Kashmir, *Roots of Conflict, Paths to Peace* (Cambridge: Harvard University Press, 2003).

[10] This is where the phrase "third world" comes from. For more information on the third-world movement, see Vijay Prashad, *The Darker Nations: A People's History of the Third World* (New York: The New Press, 2007).

[11] Neville Maxwell, "Sino-Indian Border Dispute Reconsidered," *Economic and Political Weekly* 34, no. 15 (April 10, 1999): 905–918; Ramachandra Guha, *India after Gandhi: The History of the World's Largest Democracy* (New York: Harper Collins, 2007), 306–341.

## CHAPTER 7

[1] Benjamin Robert Siegel, *Hungry Nation: Food, Famine, and the Making of Modern India* (Cambridge: Cambridge University Press, 2018).

[2] Maurice Zinkin, "Glimpses of Cooperative Farming in India and States' Finances in India: A Perspective Study for the Plan Periods," *International Affairs* 44, no.4 (October 1968): 821–822.

[3] Ashis Nandy, "Dams and Dissent: India's First Modern Environmental Activist and His Critique of the DVC Project," *Futures* 33, no. 8–9 (October 2001): 709–731.

[4] Raymond F. Hopkins, "Reform in the International Food Aid Regime: The Role of Consensual Knowledge," *International Organization* 46, no.1 (Winter 1992): 225–264.

[5] Ray Offenheiser, "The Green Revolution: Norman Borlaug and the Race to Fight Global Hunger," PBS American Experience, https://www.pbs.org/wgbh/americanexperience/features/green-revolution-norman-borlaug-race-to-fight-global-hunger/.

[6] Vandana Shiva, *The Violence of the Green Revolution: Third World Agriculture, Ecology, and Politics* (London: Zed Books, 1991).

[7] Raj Patel, "Caught Up in the War on Communism: Norman Borlaug and the 'Green Revolution,'" PBS American Experience, https://www.pbs.org/wgbh/americanexperience/features/caught-war-on-communism-norman-borlaug-and-green-revolution/.

[8] Indira Gandhi is not related to Mohandas "Mahatma" Gandhi.

[9] Zoya Hasan, "History Headline: 1971 and Now, a Tale of Slogans," *India Express*, April 14, 2019, https://indianexpress.com/article/opinion/columns/history-headline-1971-elections-2019-indira-gandhi-congress-narendra-modi-bjp-lok-sabha-polls-2019-5674388/.

[10] Bernard D'Mello, *India after Naxalbari: Unfinished History* (New York: Monthly Review Press, 2018).

[11] Nandita Gandhi, *When the Rolling Pins Hit the Streets: Women in the Anti-Price Rise Movement in Maharashtra* (New Delhi, Kali for Women, 1996).

[12] "Mother Teresa: Facts," The Nobel Prize, https://www.nobelprize.org/prizes/peace/1979/teresa/facts/; "Mother Teresa," Biography, https://www.biography.com/religious-figures/mother-teresa.

[13] Feroz Ahmed, Aijaz Ahmad, and Eqbal Ahmad, "Pakistan, Bangladesh, India: 1970–1973," *MERIP Reports* 16 (April 1973): 6–11.

[14] Ramachandra Guha, *India after Gandhi: The History of the World's Largest Democracy* (New York: Harper Collins, 2007).

[15] Gyan Prakash, *Emergency Chronicles: Indira Gandhi and Democracy's Turning Point* (Princeton: Princeton University Press, 2019).

[16] Christophe Jaffrelot and Pratinav Anil, *India's First Dictatorship: The Emergency, 1975–1977* (Oxford: Oxford University Press, 2020).

[17] Radhika Chopra, "Commemorating Hurt: Memorializing Operation Bluestar," *Skih Formations: Religion, Culture, Theory* 6, no. 2 (2010): 119–152.

[18] Uma Chakravarti, "Victims, 'Neighbours,' and 'Watan': Survivors of Anti-Sikh Carnage of 1984," *Economic and Political Weekly* 29, no. 42 (October 15, 1994): 2722–2726.

## CHAPTER 8

[1] Nimish Adhia, "The History of Economic Development in India since Independence," *Education about Asia* 23, no. 3 (Winter 2015): 18–22.

[2] Nimish Adhia, "The History of Economic Development in India since Independence."

[3] Ashok Kotwal, Bharat Ramaswami, and Wilima Wadhwa, "Economic Liberalization and Indian Economic Growth: What's the Evidence?" *Journal of Economic Literature* 49, no. 4 (December 2011): 1152–1199.

[4] A. R. Vasavi, *Shadow Spaces: Suicides and the Predicament of Rural India* (New Delhi: Three Essay Collective, 2012).

[5] Maitreesh Ghatak, "India's Inequality Problem," *India Forum*, June 23, 2021, https://www.theindiaforum.in/article/does-india-have-inequality-problem#:~:text=Since%201991%2C%20the%20year%20of,a%20mere%202.8%25%20in%202020.

[6] Ravinder Kaur, "'I Am India Shining': The Investor-Citizen and the Indelible Icon of Good Times," *Journal of Asian Studies* 75, no. 3 (August 2016): 621–648; https://www.cambridge.org/core/journals/journal-of-asian-studies/article/abs/i-am-india-shining-investor-citizen-and-the-indelible-icon-of-good-times/8C3F4119A5213DB03C5DF693935EA2F5.

[7] Shan Li and Vibhuti Agarwal, "What's Holding Back India's Economic Ambitions?" *Wall Street Journal*, August 18, 2023, https://www.wsj.com/world/india/india-economy-women-work-labor-46bfb0f0.

[8] Vandana Shiva, *The Violence of the Green Revolution: Third World Agriculture, Ecology, and Politics* (London: Zed Books, 1991); Dominique Lapierre and Javier Moro, *Five Past Midnight in Bhopal: The Epic Story of the World's Deadliest Industrial Disaster* (New York: Hachette Books, 2009); Barie Carmichael and Brian Moriarty, "How Coca-Cola Came to Terms with Its Own Water Crisis," *Washington Post*, May 31, 2018, https://www.washingtonpost.com/news/business/wp/2018/05/31/how-coca-cola-came-to-terms-with-its-own-water-crisis/.

[9] Arundhati Roy, *Power Politics* (Cambridge: South End Press, 2002); Ken Schoolland, "Property Rights and One Indian Village: Reform, Enterprise, and Dignity," *Education about Asia* 20, no. 3 (Winter 2005), https://www.asianstudies.org/publications/eaa/archives/property-rights-and-one-indian-village-reform-enterprise-and-dignity/.

[10] Jyoti Punwani, "L. K. Advani Led BJP's Hindu Nationalism Movement in 80s, 90s; Espousing Diversity Now Won't Erase His Past," *First Post*, April 7, 2019, https://www.firstpost.com/politics/lk-advani-led-bjps-hindu-nationalism movement in-80s90s-espousing diversity now won't erase his past-anti-muslim-campaign-6402631.html.

[11] The Wire Staff, "Babri Masjid: The Timeline of a Demolition," *The Wire*, September 30, 2020, https://thewire.in/communalism/babri-masjid-the-timeline-of-a-demolition.

[12] The Wire Staff, "Babri Masjid: The Timeline of a Demolition."

[13] Valay Singh, *Ayodhya: City of Faith, City of Discord* (New Delhi: Aleph Book Company, 2018).

[14] Sylvie Guichard, *The Construction of History and Nationalism in India: Textbooks, Controversies, and Politics* (London: Routledge, 2010).

[15] The Nanavati-Mehta Commission Report can be accessed here: "Commission of Inquiry (Godhra and Post Godhra Riots in Gujarat)," https://cms.neva.gov.in/FileStructure_GJ/Notices/4e7714ec-1472-490d-98ae-3a307fcef10d.pdf; The Banerjee Commission Report can be accessed here: "Report of Justice U. C. Banerjee Commission on Godhra Incident," Parliament of India, Lok Sabha Digital Library, https://eparlib.nic.in/handle/123456789/726874.

[16] Christophe Jaffrelot, "Communal Riots in Gujarat: The State at Risk?" *Heidelberg Papers in South Asian and Comparative Politics*, Working Paper #3, July 2003, https://archiv.ub.uni-heidelberg.de/volltextserver/4127/1/hpsacp17.pdf.

[17] "Timeline of the Riots in Modi's Gujarat," *New York Times*, August 19, 2005, nytimes.com/interactive/2014/04/06/world/asia/modi-gujarat-riots-timeline.html#/#time287_11074.

[18] Randeep Ramesh, "Surprise Landslide in Indian State Election," *Guardian*, May 12, 2007, https://www.theguardian.com/world/2007/may/12/india.randeepramesh.

[19] Durba Mitra and Mrinal Satish, "Testing Chastity, Evidencing Rape: Impact of Medical Jurisprudence on Rape Adjudication in India," *Economic and Political Weekly* 49, no. 41 (October 11, 2014): 51–58, https://www.jstor.org/stable/24480853?casa_token=QKMpZrxjs0UAAAAA%3AupLh3D0vs-j1n80Y4DJ73JeNpDGwVlp7zRtmhgyztbHJDjgfJLhS9AGKOwg7s4YG1QhEwkKqpNEhSBaTDgAgPboO-MwN1z5TU1VyFKuQPHKMLS2Vaw&seq=2.

[20] Danish Sheikh, *Love and Reparation: A Theatrical Response to the Section 377 Litigation in India* (Kolkata: Seagull Books, 2021).

[21] Duncan McDuie-Ra, "Fifty-Year Disturbance: The Armed Forces Special Powers Act and Exceptionalism in a South Asian Periphery," *Contemporary South Asia* 17, no. 3 (September 2009): 255–270; Emily Rook-Koepsel, "Dissenting against the Defence of India Rules: Emergency Regulations and the Space of Extreme Government Action," *South Asia: Journal of South Asian Studies* 41, no. 3 (August 2018): 642–657.

## CONCLUSION

[1] Lucien Ellington and Savannah Mason, "The Modi Government and Religious Freedom," *Education about Asia* 28, no. 2 (Fall 2023); The Wire Staff, "The Updated List of India's 'Antinationals' (According to Modi's Government)," *The Wire*, February 19, 2021, https://thewire.in/rights/india-modi-anti-national-protest-arrest-sedition-authoritarianism.

[2] Isaac Chotiner, "A Kashmiri Novelist on a State under Siege," *New Yorker*, August 16, 2019, https://www.newyorker.com/news/q-and-a/a-kashmiri-novelist-on-a-state-under-siege; Arundhati Roy, "Walking with the Comrades," *Outlook Magazine*, April 26, 2016, https://www.outlookindia.com/magazine/story/walking-with-the-comrades/264738.

[3] "India: Events of 2018," Human Rights Watch World Report 2019, https://www.hrw.org/world-report/2019/country-chapters/india.

[4] "India: Events of 2018," Human Rights Watch World Report 2019.

[5] "Who Gets to Breathe Clean Air in New Delhi?" *New York Times*, December 17, 2020, https://www.nytimes.com/interactive/2020/12/17/world/asia/india-pollution-inequality.html.

[6] "History of BRICS," BRICS, https://infobrics.org/page/history-of-brics/.

[7] Daniel Markey and Andrew Scobell, "Three Things to Know about China-India Tensions," *United States Institute of Peace*, October 19, 2023, https://www.usip.org/publications/2023/10/three-things-know-about-china-india-tensions.

[8] "India: Arrests of Activists Politically Motivated," Human Rights Watch, September 16, 2020, https://www.hrw.org/news/2020/09/16/india-arrests-activists-politically-motivated; "2022 Report on International Religious Freedom: India," United States Department of State, https://www.state.gov/reports/2022-report-on-international-religious-freedom/india/#:~:text=The%20U.S.%20government%20estimates%20the,%3B%20and%20Sikhs%2C%201.7%20percent.

[9] Richard H. Davis, *Global India circa 100 CE: South Asia in World History* (Ann Arbor: Association for Asian Studies), 18 and 66.

[10] Ariana Monique Salazar, "8 Key Findings about Christians in India," Pew Research Center, July 12, 2021, https://www.pewresearch.org/short-reads/2021/07/12/8-key-findings-about-christians-in-india/.

[11] "India," Freedom House, https://freedomhouse.org/country/india.

# GLOSSARY

**Adivasi**: Indigenous people of India, often also referred to as "scheduled tribes." Adivasis make up just over 8 percent of the Indian population. There are as many as five hundred different groups that fall under the terms "Adivasi" or "scheduled tribes."

**All-India Muslim League**: Founded in 1906, the All-India Muslim League was a political organization devoted to securing rights and equality for Indian Muslims. After 1940, the All-India Muslim League began advocating for a separate Muslim state in South Asia called Pakistan.

**Ambedkar, Bhimrao**: Dr. Bhimrao Ambedkar was the most prominent Dalit-rights activist from the 1920s until his death in 1956. His writings about Dalit rights and politics are still important today. In addition to his work for Dalit rights, Dr. Ambedkar was the first law minister of India and the chief writer of the Indian constitution.

**British East India Company**: A company founded in 1600 in England for the purpose of managing the British trade with India. The British East India Company governed India on behalf of the British government until after the First War for Indian Independence in 1857, after which the British government began to directly administer India.

**Caste System**: A hierarchical system of organization of Hindus that determines a person's appropriate work and duty by birth. Although technically only religious in nature, caste hierarchies extend into the systematic oppression of lower-caste and Dalit people throughout Indian life. The constitution formally banned the caste system and the practice of caste restrictions, but caste continues to play an important and highly discriminatory role in Indian life today.

**Civil Disobedience**: Civil disobedience, also called Satyagraha, was the term used for Gandhi's form of nonviolent protest against colonial rule. Following civil disobedience meant a nonviolent refusal to follow laws or customs that reinforced colonial rule while willfully suffering the consequences of this refusal.

**Company Raj**: The term for the British East India Company administration. "Raj" means "rule," so the Company Raj was the rule of the company.

**Constituent Assembly**: The Constituent Assembly was organized in 1946 to draft and ratify a constitution for an independent India. Once the constitution was ratified, the Constituent Assembly became the provisional legislature until elections were held in 1952.

**Dalit**: Term for the lowest caste designation. Often, Dalits are perceived to be outside the caste system and therefore polluting to Hindus. As part of the caste hierarchy, Dalits often did jobs related to excrement, animal carcasses, human remains, and garbage. Dalits have been systematically and severely oppressed in India and remain the targets of systematic and direct discrimination today.

**Economic Liberalization**: In 1991, the Indian government shifted from a highly regulated economy that severely limited foreign investment, imposed high tariffs on imports, and controlled manufacturing to an economy with fewer regulations and more openness to private and foreign investment.

**Emergency**: The period between 1975 and 1977, when Prime Minister Indira Gandhi suspended the government, squashed civil rights, and made mass arrests of political opponents. It ended in 1977, when Gandhi reinstated the government, called for new elections, and allowed for a peaceful transfer of power.

**First War of Indian Independence**: Also called the Indian Mutiny, the Revolt of 1857, and the Rebellion of 1857. Some Indian British East India Company soldiers allied with armies from princely states, and some provinces joined together to end British rule in India and reinstate the Mughal emperor. The fighting lasted for more than two years. After the British had defeated the Indian forces, the British government removed the British East India Company from governing in India and placed the Indian colony under the direct management of the British government.

**Gandhi, Mohandas "Mahatma"**: Mohandas Gandhi, often called "Mahatma" (great saint), was a leader of Indian independence movements from 1909 until his assassination in 1948. He was an Indian National Congress leader. Gandhi theorized many political resistance strategies that remain important, including the need for nonviolent civil disobedience.

**Green Revolution**: Begun in the 1940s in Mexico, the Green Revolution was focused on creating high-yielding food grains. In 1967, after several years of bad growing seasons due to famine, the Indian government began promoting and subsidizing the use of Green Revolution seeds and technology to produce more food.

**Hindu Nationalism**: Also called Hindutva, Hindu nationalism is the belief that India is a Hindu nation and that non-Hindus either do not belong, or must learn to live in, a Hindu state.

**Indian National Congress**: Begun in 1885, the Indian National Congress Party was the most prominent anti-colonial organizing party until independence and became the dominant political party in India until the early 1990s. Congress continues to be one of the two main political parties in India, occupying the center-left political affiliation.

**Line of Control**: The de facto Kashmiri border between India and Pakistan. The Line of Control was set after the 1948 Indo-Pak war and has remained relatively consistent and consistently disputed ever since.

**Mughal Empire**: Begun in 1526, when Babur defeated the Delhi sultanates, the Mughal Empire technically lasted until 1859. From 1765 until 1859, the empire only had ceremonial power. At its height in 1707, the Mughal Empire ruled roughly 80 percent of the Indian subcontinent.

**Naxalbari/Naxalite**: Naxalbari is the site of a 1967 revolt by Indian Maoists hoping to challenge the Indian state. After the unsuccessful 1967 revolt, leaders of the movement, called Naxalites, have continued to violently agitate against the Indian government. Naxalite activity is most common in the poorest regions of India.

**Nehru, Jawaharlal**: The first prime minister of India, Nehru was a leader of the Congress Party before independence. He died in 1964.

**Pakistan**: Pakistan was formed in 1947 upon the independence and partition of India. India was partitioned into two countries along religious lines—India in the predominantly Hindu regions and Pakistan in the predominantly Muslim areas.

**Partition**: At independence, the British divided India into two countries on the basis of religious majority. Pakistan was formed by the Muslim-majority provinces in the west and the east, and India was the middle section. More than fifteen million people migrated across borderlines, often fleeing from communal violence. More than one million people died during the riots surrounding the partition.

**Swadeshi Movement**: Begun after the 1905 partition of Bengal, the Swadeshi movement encouraged people to buy Indian-made goods and boycott the British in order to achieve Indian home rule.

**Total Revolution**: The Total Revolution Movement, alternatively called the Bihar Movement and the J. P. Movement, was begun by J. P. Narayan as a protest against corruption in government. Indira Gandhi named it as one of the reasons for imposing emergency.

**Zamindari System**: Zamindars, or landowners, were granted extremely large tracts of lands and authorized to set taxes on these lands, becoming de facto rulers. Under the zamindari system, in addition to taxes and rents, zamindars often required a certain percentage of their tenant's labor. The zamindari system was abolished in the Indian constitution.

# SUGGESTIONS FOR FURTHER READING

Alam, Muzaffar and Sanjay Subrahmanyam. *Writing the Mughal World: Studies on Culture and Politics*. New York: Columbia University Press, 2012.

Ambedkar, B. R. *The Essential Ambedkar*. Edited by Bhalchandra Mungekar. New Delhi: Rupa, 2017.

Bandyopadhyay, Sekhar, ed., *The Nationalist Movement in India: A Reader*. New Delhi: Oxford University Press, 2009.

Bose, Sugata, and Ayesha Jalal. *Modern South Asia: History, Culture, and Political Economy*. 5th ed. London: Routledge, 2022.

Butalia, Urvashi. *The Other Side of Silence: Voices from the Partition of India*. Durham: Duke University Press, 2000.

Chaudhuri, K. N. *Trade and Civilization in the Indian Ocean: An Economic History from the Rise of Islam to 1750*. Cambridge: Cambridge University Press, 1985.

De, Rohit. *A People's Constitution: The Everyday Life of Law in the Indian Republic*. Princeton: Princeton University Press, 2018.

Gandhi, M. K. *Hind Swaraj and Other Writings*. Edited by Anthony Parel. Cambridge: Cambridge University Press, 2009.

Guha, Ramachandra. *India after Gandhi: The History of the World's Largest Democracy*. New York: HarperCollins, 2007.

Jaffrelot, Christophe, ed., *Hindu Nationalism: A Reader*. Princeton: Princeton University Press, 2007.

Kaviraj, Sudipta. *The Imaginary Institutions of India: Politics and Ideas*. New York: Columbia University Press, 2010.

Keating, Christine. *Decolonizing Democracy: Transforming the Social Contract in India*. University Park: Pennsylvania State University Press, 2011.

Khan, Yasmin. *The Great Partition: The Making of India and Pakistan*. New Haven: Yale University Press, 2007.

Metcalf, Barbara and Thomas Metcalf. *A Concise History of Modern India.* Cambridge: Cambridge University Press, 2001.

Narayan, Jayaprakash. *Prison Diary.* Seattle: University of Washington Press, 1978.

Nehru, Jawaharlal. *The Discovery of India.* New Delhi: Penguin Books India, 2004.

O'Hanlon, Rosalind. *Caste, Conflict, and Ideology: Mahatma Jyotirao Phule and Low-Caste Protest in Nineteenth-Century Western India.* Cambridge: Cambridge University Press, 1985.

Prakash, Gyan. *Emergency Chronicles: Indira Gandhi and Democracy's Turning Point.* Princeton: Princeton University Press, 2019.

Prashad, Vijay. *The Darker Nations: A People's History of the Third World.* New York: The New Press, 2007.

Richards, John F. *The Mughal Empire.* Cambridge: Cambridge University Press, 1995.

Sarkar, Sumit and Tanika Sarkar, eds. *Women and Social Reform in Modern India: A Reader.* Bloomington: Indiana University Press, 2008.

Sen, Amartya. *The Argumentative Indian: Writings on Indian History, Culture, and Identity.* New York: Farrar, Straus, and Giroux, 2005.

Siegel, Benjamin Robert. *Hungry Nation: Food, Famine, and the Making of Modern India.* Cambridge: Cambridge University Press, 2018.